GREATways to Teach and Learn™

Connect with Reading
Grade 3

Written by

Patricia Pedigo and Roger DeSanti

Edited and produced by
Patricia Pedigo

©2008 Plutarch Publications, Inc. PPI -1003

ISBN 978-1-934990-07-0

GREATways to Teach and Learn: Connect with Reading Grade 3
Published by
Plutarch Publications, Inc.
U.S.A.
Email (for customer service enquires): plutarch_inc@yahoo.com
Copyright© 2008 Plutarch Publications, Inc.

Copyright © 2008, Plutarch Publications, Inc., Mandeville, Louisiana. All rights reserved. The purchase of this material entitles the buyer to reproduce worksheets and activities for classroom use only—not for commercial resale. Reproduction of these materials for an entire school or district is prohibited. No part of this book may be reproduced (except as noted above), stored in a retrieval system, or transmitted in any form or by any means (mechanically, electronically, recording, etc.) without the prior written consent of Plutarch Publications, Inc.

ISBN-13: 978-1-934990-07-0
ISBN-10: 1-934990-07-8

About the series ...

The GREATways to Teach and Learn™ series are books intended to supplement curriculum and textbooks. Over sixty pages of activities presented in each GREATways to Teach and Learn™ book engage the learner in active practice of basic skills required at the appropriate grade level. Activities are designed with various learning styles in mind to include every child in the learning process.

Each book contains two pages of *Quick Cues,* a handy list of important vocabulary, rules, or examples of standards covered in that GREATways to Teach and Learn™ book. The page "How to Use This Book" provides suggestions and ideas for using *Quick Cues* for additional instruction or practice.

GREATways to Teach and Learn™ books are designed to comply with State Curriculum Standards. Although the level at which specific topics are mandated may vary from State to State, many State Curriculum Standards agree on the grade level at which most skills are introduced. The GREATways to Teach and Learn™ series focuses on those standards that are commonly introduced at each grade level. The Score Computation Chart (page 4) and the Standards Competency Chart (page 5) provide a viable means to assess the level at which a child is able to complete each standard presented.

The goal of this series is to provide grade appropriate standards, practice, and application in a straight-forward, easy to understand manner. Appropriate materials and presentation produce comprehension. Practice produces proficiency. Application produces students able to interact with the real world.

About the authors and editor .....

Patricia Pedigo, **M.Ed.** in elementary education, also earned the Reading Specialist endorsement. She has more than 20 years experience in elementary and junior high classrooms and a passion for working with "learning different" children. Patricia has authored and/or edited 50 instructional books that are used in classrooms across North America.

Roger DeSanti Sr., Ed.D. in Reading and Special Education, is a Professor of Education whose area of expertise is literacy and the learning process. He has over 30 years of classroom experience working with and educating children and their teachers. Roger has over 100 publications, including instructional books that are used in classrooms across North America.

Connect With Reading Grade 3

How to Use This Book	1
Quick Cues Vocabulary	2
Quick Cues Vocabulary	3
Score Computation Chart	4
Standards Competency Chart	5

Vocabulary

Word Identification	6
Word Identification	7
Word Identification	8
Synonyms	9
Synonyms	10
Synonyms	11
Antonyms	12
Antonyms	13
Antonyms	14
Categorize	15
Categorize	16
Categorize	17

Decoding Skills

Prefixes	18
Prefixes	19
Prefixes	20
Suffixes	21
Suffixes	22
Suffixes	23
Figurative Language	24
Figurative Language	25
Context Clues	26
Context Clues	27
Context Clues	28
Context Clues	29

Concept Building

Sequence of Events	30
Sequence of Events	31
Referents	32
Referents	33
Compare/Contrast	34
Compare/Contrast	35
Compare/Contrast	36
Cause and Effect	37
Cause and Effect	38
Conclude/Predict	39
Conclude/Predict	40
Author's Purpose	41
Genre	42

Comprehension *Narrative Stories*

Matt in Iowa	43
Isabela in Arizona	44
Ben in Florida	45
Winona in South Dakota	46
Vinnie in New York	47
Susan in Kansas	48
Chelsea in Maine	49
Clyde in Tennessee	50
Inola in North Carolina	51

Comprehension *Expository Stories*

Inventions	52
Balloons	53
Can Opener	54
Dishwasher	55
Flashlight	56
Lawn Mower	57
Paperclip	58
Straws	59
Umbrella	60

Comprehension

Maps/Charts	61
Maps/Charts	62
Maps/Charts	63
Forms/Signs	64
Forms/Signs	65
Forms or Signs	66
Dictionary/Glossary	67
Dictionary/Glossary	68
Dictionary/Glossary	69

Answer Keys

Pages 6 - 9	70	Pages 38 - 41	78
Pages 10 - 13	71	Pages 42 - 45	79
Pages 14 - 17	72	Pages 46 - 49	80
Pages 18 - 21	73	Pages 50 - 53	81
Pages 22 - 25	74	Pages 54 - 57	82
Pages 26 - 29	75	Pages 58 - 61	83
Pages 30 - 33	76	Pages 62 - 65	84
Pages 34 - 37	77	Pages 66 - 69	85

©2008 Plutarch Publications, Inc. PPI -1003

How to use this book ...

GREATways: Instruction books offer several features designed to enhance the learning process and assist the teacher in assessing the learner's progress. On the next few pages you will find Quick Cues, a Score Computation Chart, a Standards Competency Chart, and recommendations based on the competency level of the learner.

QUICK CUES: This book includes two pages of *Quick Cues* which are important facts at your fingertips. The Quick Cues found on pages two and three of this book lists 160 words that should be part of the basic reading vocabulary of third grade learners. Ways to use these pages are as varied as the number of readers, but here are a few suggestions to get started:

- Have the learner scan a newspaper or magazine and try to find words from the *Quick Cues* list.
- Create a "Book of Words" where the learner places a word from the list on each page and adds an illustration
- Ask the learner to select ten of the words and use them in a story
- List each word on an index card and use them as flashcards. The learner can keep the words that are correctly identified.
- Create a "Word Bank" box where the flashcards can be kept. Have the learner use these words to create sentences or short stories.

SCORE COMPUTATION CHART: This assessment tool can be found on page four of this book. After the learner completes an activity in this book, record the number of correct items on the score computation chart. When all pages for a listed standard have been completed, tally the number of correct answers and record it in the column on the far right (under the total of correct answers possible). Transfer the learner's totals to the chart on page five to find the level of competency.

STANDARDS COMPETENCY CHART: Use the total number correct scores from page four to identify the level at which the learner comprehends/applies the standard. The range of scores within each level (Mastery, Instructional, Basic, and Limited) are approximate indicators of how well the learner understands and can apply each standard. The degree of competency at that level will vary with the score. For example, a score of 54 in Prefix/Suffix indicates Mastery, but is close to Instructional and the learner could benefit from more practice with that standard. Recommendations based on the competency level are offered at the bottom of the page.

Quick Cues
Third Grade Word List

actual	cause	design	fame
admire	celebrate	difficult	fellow
adventure	celery	dine	fierce
allow	cellar	disappear	firm
amaze	charm	display	flare
ancient	chart	dozen	flashing
anxious	coast	droop	flight
attach	computer	eager	forest
autumn	conclusion	effect	friendship
awful	continue	elbow	fuss
banana	costume	emergency	future
beneath	couple	enclose	gentle
birdhouse	cousin	entire	grapes
blaze	curtain	entrance	grin
boast	customer	excited	grumpy
borrow	damp	excuse	guest
breathe	dangerous	fail	guide
bubbles	depend	faint	hatch
cape	dependable	fairy	helmet
carrot	desert	fake	imaginary

©2008 Plutarch Publications, Inc. PPI-1003

Quick Cues

Third Grade Word List

impolite	naughty	quarter	struck
impossible	necessary	rapid	swift
inch	nervous	reason	theater
instrument	nonstop	receive	thread
invention	ocean	remove	timid
jacket	odd	rescue	title
jewel	operate	restaurant	tomato
journey	ordinary	safety	traveler
knife	palace	sausage	twist
lettuce	parent	scarf	underwater
magical	peach	scrub	unwrap
map	pebble	sequence	valley
mend	pleasant	serve	vanish
mention	polite	shallow	visitor
misbehave	pollution	shiver	wand
mistake	potato	siren	weep
mountain	powerful	skeleton	windowsill
mouth	prevent	sled	wobble
musical	proud	straw	wooden
nature	purpose	stream	yawn

©2008 Plutarch Publications, Inc. PPI-1003

Score Computation Chart

Connect with Reading

Grade 3

Word Identification											Score
Page number	6	7	8	15	16	17					
# possible	16	16	16	18	18	18					102
# correct											

Synonym/Antonym											
Page number	9	10	11	12	13	14					
# possible	12	12	12	12	12	12					72
# correct											

Prefix/Suffix											
Page number	18	19	20	21	22	23					
# possible	10	10	10	10	10	10					60
# correct											

Context Clues											
Page number	24	25	26	27	28	29					
# possible	6	6	10	10	10	10					52
# correct											

Sequence/Referents											
Page number	30	31	32	33							
# possible	16	16	14	8							54
# correct											

Compare/Contrast											
Page number	34	35	36								
# possible	15	15	15								45
# correct											

Cause/Effect/Predict											
Page number	37	38	39	40							
# possible	12	12	4	4							32
# correct											

Purpose/Genre											
Page number	41	42									
# possible	20	6									26
# correct											

Narrative Story											
Page number	43	44	45	46	47	48	49	50	51		
# possible	8	8	8	8	8	8	8	8	8		72
# correct											

Expository Story											
Page number	52	53	54	55	56	57	58	59	60		
# possible	10	11	10	11	10	11	11	10	11		95
# correct											

Functional Context											
Page number	61	62	63	64	65	66	67	68	69		
# possible	12	11	12	6	9	12	26	8	8		104
# correct											

©2008 Plutarch Publications, Inc. PPI -1003

Standards Competency Chart

Step 1: After the learner completes each page, record the number correct on the Score Computation Chart (page 4). Calculate the total number correct for each standard.

Step 2: Find the learner's score for each standard in the boxes of that row. Mark the box with an X (or the learner's score) to identify the level of competency for that standard. For example, a score of 60 for the standard of Synonym/Antonym places the child on the "Instructional" level and a score of 68 would indicate the "Mastery" level.

Step 3: Follow the recommendation guidelines at the bottom of this page.

Standard	Mastery	Instructional	Basic	Limited
Word Identification	102 - 92	91 - 77	76 - 61	60 or below
Synonym/Antonym	72 - 65	64 - 54	53 - 43	42 or below
Prefix/Suffix	60 - 54	53 - 45	44 - 36	35 or below
Context Clues	52 - 47	46 - 39	38 - 31	30 or below
Sequence/Referents	54 - 49	48 - 40	39 - 32	31 or below
Compare/Contrast	45 - 41	40 - 34	33 - 27	26 or below
Cause/Effect/Predict	32 - 29	28 - 24	23 - 19	18 or below
Purpose/Genre	26 - 24	23 - 20	19 - 15	14 or below
Narrative Passage	72 - 65	64 - 54	53 - 43	42 or below
Expository Passage	95 - 86	85 - 71	70 - 57	56 or below
Functional Passage	104 - 94	93 - 78	77 - 62	61 or below

Recommendation Guidelines

Mastery: The learner is capable of using this standard independently. Move on to the next higher grade level.

Instructional: The learner has a working understanding of the standard, but needs some guided practice on this grade level.

Basic: The learner has minimal grasp of the standard and needs direct instruction and guided practice to apply the concept fully. The learner could benefit from moving one grade level lower for review and extra practice before approaching the standard at this level once again.

Limited: The learner has a limited understanding of the standard and should be moved to the next lower grade level for instruction and practice.

©2008 Plutarch Publications, Inc. PPI -1003

Name _____   Standard: Word Identification

Look at each picture. Circle the word in each row that describes the picture. There are four words for each picture.

1. curtain   couple   costume
2. cape   cabin   ceiling
3. soldier   skeleton   solve
4. hoof   helpful   Halloween

1. sled   basket   bicycle
2. juice   jacket   June
3. scissors   sting   scarf
4. angry   excited   gruff

1. hive   package   birdhouse
2. goose   bluebird   berry
3. weep   wooden   wade
4. flight   fossil   firefly

1. unwrap   unlock   underwater
2. grape   goldfish   giraffe
3. barrel   bubbles   braid
4. breathe   broom   banana

©2008 Plutarch Publications, Inc. PPI -1003

Name _____   Standard: Word Identification

Look at each picture. Circle the word in each row that describes the picture. There are four words for each picture.

1. blaze   bulb   brass
2. hose   hotel   heart
3. flute   fireman   fireplace
4. equal   eagle   emergency

1. whip   wedding   windowsill
2. curb   comb   curtain
3. autumn   apron   avenue
4. engine   elbow   eighty

1. puddle   potato   pilot
2. ticket   tide   tomato
3. lamp   lettuce   lizard
4. club   closet   carrot

1. fern   flashing footstep
2. pad   pebble   policeman
3. siren   slice   swamp
4. attic   airport   automobile

©2008 Plutarch Publications, Inc. PPI-1003   7

Name _____   Standard: Word Identification

Look at each picture. Circle the word in each row that describes the picture. There are four words for each picture.

1. fairy   fasten   fiddle
2. woven   wand   waterfall
3. male   material   magical
4. cousin   china   charming

1. museum   musical   maple
2. trumpet   timid   thousand
3. inch   include   instrument
4. mouth   mystery   million

1. rescue   reader   restaurant
2. medal   math   meal
3. serve   system   startle
4. dine   danger   develop

1. banana   ballet   beard
2. gaze   guest   grapes
3. pause   peach   polite
4. braid   bowl   balance

Name _____   Standard: Synonyms

SYNONYMS are words that have almost the **same meaning**. Circle the word or phrase that is a synonym for the underlined word in each sentence.

1. She likes to <u>grin</u> when she is happy.
 	
   smile   **frown**
 	
        sway
	2. The jello is <u>firm</u> and ready to eat.
	
	   soft **marble**
	
	        hard

3. Please <u>remove</u> your hat when you are inside the house.
 	
  throw away   **take off**
 	
      put on
	4. We had a <u>pleasant</u> visit with grandmother today.
	
	   nice **floppy**
	
	      graceful

5. Will your parents <u>allow</u> you to spend the night at my house?
 	
   let   **stop**
 	
      match
	6. The flag will <u>droop</u> if it gets wet.
	
	   fasten **sag**
	
	      mend

7. The furnace is in the <u>cellar</u>.
 	
   attic   **tank**
 	
      basement
	8. Lightening <u>struck</u> that old tree.
	
	   hit **startled**
	
	      yank

9. What is the <u>title</u> of that book?
 	
   artist   **name**
 	
      record
	10. <u>Whip</u> the eggs before you add them to the cake mix.
	
	   beat **squeeze**
	
	      sort

11. I have a <u>pebble</u> in my shoe.
 	
   tongue   **saucer**
 	
      stone
	12. Who is the <u>author</u> of that book?
	
	   suspect **customer**
	
	      writer

©2008 Plutarch Publications, Inc. PPI -1003

Name _____   Standard: Synonyms

SYNONYMS are words that have almost the **same meaning**. Circle the word or phrase that is a synonym for the underlined word in each sentence.

1. That sandwich tasted <u>horrible</u>! **delicious** **awful** **favor**	2. Kyle mowed his <u>lawn</u> last Saturday. **grass** **chimney** **driveway**
3. Wear a <u>jacket</u> because it is chilly today. **example** **coat** **buggy**	4. Brandon likes to <u>boast</u> about his soccer awards. **brag** **suggest** **polish**
5. I would like a <u>couple</u> of cookies please. **three** **two** **none**	6. Mother got a <u>dozen</u> roses from Father. **split** **twelve** **thoughtful**
7. Joey left his clothes in a <u>heap</u> on the floor. **pile** **drain** **laundry**	8. Please <u>attach</u> this page to your test. **hush** **fasten** **nibble**
9. Can you give me a <u>hint</u> about what my present will be? **wrap** **remind** **clue**	10. That wind feels <u>icy</u> today, so wear a scarf. **cold** **stubborn** **worse**
11. Can you <u>mend</u> the broken fence? **repair** **swirl** **pinch**	12. Who will <u>paddle</u> the canoe across the lake? **remove** **burst** **row**

©2008 Plutarch Publications, Inc. PPI-1003

Name _____ Standard: Synonyms

SYNONYMS are words that have almost the **same meaning**. Circle the word or phrase that is a synonym for the underlined word in each sentence.

1. I made a <u>stupid</u> mistake on this test.

    expert   **dumb**

    design

2. Kelly's mother will <u>guide</u> us to the park.

    lead   **demand**

    hatch

3. I am tired so it is time to <u>quit</u> working on this project.

    begin   **stop**

    form

4. The car has a <u>powerful</u> engine that makes it go fast!

    brass   **crisp**

    strong

5. Be <u>gentle</u> when you pet the puppy.

    rough   **tender**

    marvelous

6. Did that wet vase <u>harm</u> the finish on the wooden table?

    hurt   **label**

    obey

7. We need special <u>equipment</u> to cut down this tree.

    tools   **fireworks**

    patterns

8. Sonja's family went to the <u>coast</u> for their vacation.

    gym   **museum**

    seashore

9. The men found some <u>ancient</u> arrowheads in that field.

    object   **dangerous**

    old

10. I <u>weep</u> when I peel onions!

    bleed   **cry**

    study

11. We had a <u>visitor</u> in our classroom today.

    guest   **servant**

    poet

12. My grandfather told me a <u>tale</u> of when he was a boy.

    telescope   **fountain**

    story

Name _____   Standard: Antonyms

ANTONYMS are words that have **opposite meanings**. Circle the word or phrase that is an antonym for the underlined word in each sentence.

1. Three is an <u>odd</u> number. strange double even	2. It is time to say <u>goodbye</u> and leave now. ourselves hello foolish
3. Please pass your papers <u>forward</u>. around backward serious	4. The children were <u>joyful</u> when the party started. sad slippery complete
5. You can store that box <u>beneath</u> the bed. between over safety	6. We will <u>continue</u> to play the game until someone wins. stop stumble relax
7. Is that an <u>actual</u> medal from World War II? fake true brass	8. The dogs seemed to be <u>calm</u> during the rainstorm. comfortable lazy nervous
9. Sara's clothes got a little <u>damp</u> from the rain. dry chilly popular	10. China is a country <u>faraway</u> from here. distant near private
11. Ronda has a <u>messy</u> room that needs cleaning. tasty peaceful neat	12. Will the teacher <u>excuse</u> me for being so late to school? punish suspect sparkle

Name _____   Standard: Antonyms

ANTONYMS are words that have **opposite meanings**. Circle the word or phrase that is an antonym for the underlined word in each sentence.

1. That <u>swift</u> boat won the race! 　**slow**　　　　**stray** 　　　**fisherman**	2. Those two countries are at <u>war</u> because they don't agree. 　**danger**　　　　**battle** 　　　**peace**
3. That delicious food just seemed to <u>vanish</u> from the table! 　**choke**　　　　**appear** 　　　**feast**	4. You must <u>twist</u> the wire around this peg. 　**scatter**　　　　**sweep** 　　　**straighten**
5. It shows good manners when you are <u>polite</u>. 　**rude**　　　　**thrown** 　　　**hopeful**	6. This pool is too <u>shallow</u> for diving. 　**narrow**　　　　**deep** 　　　**frozen**
7. Jan plays with her <u>imaginary</u> friend. 　**timid**　　　　**backward** 　　　**real**	8. This is just an <u>ordinary</u> pencil. 　**shaggy**　　　　**unusual** 　　　**plastic**
9. Christie wore a <u>fancy</u> new dress to the party. 　**marvelous**　　　　**plain** 　　　**gown**	10. Judy <u>lowered</u> the shades to darken the room. 　**raised**　　　　**guarded** 　　　**checked**
11. May I <u>borrow</u> that book when you are finished? 　**lend**　　　　**chose** 　　　**control**	12. Sam was <u>proud</u> that he won the contest. 　**eager**　　　　**fearful** 　　　**ashamed**

Name _____   Standard: Antonyms

ANTONYMS are words that have **opposite meanings**. Circle the word or phrase that is an antonym for the underlined word in each sentence.

1. The circus act <u>amazed</u> us with their tricks. **angered** **bored** **offered**	2. It is sometimes <u>difficult</u> to remember people's names. **easy** **enormous** **awful**
3. The class was <u>excited</u> to go on a field trip. **disappointed** **faint** **playful**	4. The chirping birds were <u>noisy</u> in the early morning. **anxious** **aloud** **quiet**
5. Daniel will <u>receive</u> a package in the mail today. **suggest** **deliver** **report**	6. The owner of the restaurant will <u>hire</u> the new waitress. **fire** **sew** **prepare**
7. The little boy was <u>grumpy</u> and needed a nap. **crabby** **thirsty** **friendly**	8. The kitchen knife was too <u>dull</u> to cut the meat. **slippery** **sharp** **usual**
9. How hot does water need to be to <u>boil</u>? **freeze** **tremble** **flutter**	10. We will go to the movie and get a pizza <u>afterward</u>. **accept** **anytime** **before**
11. The <u>attic</u> is the room at the top of the house. **chimney** **clubhouse** **basement**	12. That house is as big as a <u>palace</u>! **banquet** **barnyard** **hut**

©2008 Plutarch Publications, Inc. PPI-1003

Name _____   Standard: Categorize

The group of words below belong in a category together. Write the title of the group on the line below.

These are: _____

zebra	turtle	lion	horse
dog	ferret	parrot	goldfish
cat	rhinoceros	seal	leopard
giraffe	tiger	elephant	snake
rabbit			orangutan

Sort the words from the box into these two groups:

PETS   **FOUND IN ZOOS**

_____   _____

_____   _____

_____   _____

_____   _____

_____   _____

_____   _____

_____   _____

©2008 Plutarch Publications, Inc. PPI-1003

Name _____   Standard: Categorize

The group of words below belong in a category together. Write the title of the group on the line below.

These are: _____

beef	potato	bacon	lettuce
hamburger	steak	chicken	pork
steak	celery	corn	sausage
onion	ham	radish	turkey
carrot			squash

Sort the words from the box into two groups. Label the groups.

VEGETABLE	MEAT
_____	_____
_____	_____
_____	_____
_____	_____
_____	_____
_____	_____
_____	_____

©2008 Plutarch Publications, Inc. PPI-1003

Name _____   Standard: Categorize

The group of words below belong in a category together. Write the title of the group on the line below.

These are: _____

river	lake	field	bay
mountain	stream	sea	soil
ocean	creek	cave	forest
pond	hill	rock	desert
valley			gulf

Sort the words from the box into two groups. Label the groups.

WATER   **LAND**

_____   _____

_____   _____

_____   _____

_____   _____

_____   _____

_____   _____

_____   _____

©2008 Plutarch Publications, Inc. PPI-1003

Name _____   Standard: Prefixes

A **PREFIX** is a group of letters placed in front of a word to change the meaning of that word. Each prefix has its own meaning. For example:

"en" - to make	Enable "makes able".
"dis" - apart from, not	Distaste "does not taste good".
"un" - not	Unhappy means "not happy".
"mis" - wrong	Mistake means "take the wrong way".

Read each sentence then write the meaning of the underlined word on the blank below.

1. Matt will <u>enjoy</u> his ice cream.
   _____

2. Will this key <u>unlock</u> the door?
   _____

3. The magician will make a rabbit <u>disappear</u>!
   _____

4. Do you think it is <u>unfair</u> to have to go to bed early?
   _____

5. Please <u>enclose</u> a picture of yourself in your next letter to me.
   _____

6. Ryan <u>disabled</u> the radio when he took it apart.
   _____

7. I <u>misread</u> the map and turned on the wrong street.
   _____

8. Sylvia is <u>unlike</u> her brother in many ways.
   _____

9. Did the dog <u>misbehave</u> when you left him home alone?
   _____

10. Can you <u>unfold</u> those sheets for me?
    _____

©2008 Plutarch Publications, Inc. PPI -1003

Name _____   Standard: Prefixes

A **PREFIX** is a group of letters placed in front of a word to change the meaning of that word. Each prefix has its own meaning. For example:

"non" - not	Nonsense "makes no sense".
"re" - back or again	Regain means "to gain back".
"pre" - before	Preheat means "to heat before using".
"sub" - under	Subway means "a way under".

Read each sentence then write the meaning of the underlined word on the blank below.

1. Please refill the watering can for me.
   _____

2. We had a nonstop airplane flight to Denver.
   _____

3. I grow these submarine plants in my fish tank.
   _____

4. Shall we recount the votes to be sure who won?
   _____

5. Drinking orange juice can help prevent a cold.
   _____

6. Use the nonstick pan to fry the hamburgers.
   _____

7. I woke up predawn because I was excited about the party today.
   _____

8. I like to read nonfiction books because they are about real people.
   _____

9. Will you please return the sweater that you borrowed last week?
   _____

10. Do you recall where Sally lives?
    _____

©2008 Plutarch Publications, Inc. PPI-1003

Name _____   Standard: Prefixes

A **PREFIX** is a group of letters placed in front of a word to change the meaning of that word. Each prefix has its own meaning. For example:

"com" - with, together	Combine means "put together".
"im" - not, never	Impassable means "not able to pass".
"bi" - two	Bisect means "to cut in two pieces".
"over" - too much or across	Overused means "used too much".

Read each sentence then write the meaning of the underlined word on the blank below.

1. Did the catcher <u>overthrow</u> the ball to second base?
   _____

2. Mother <u>compresses</u> her lips when she gets angry.
   _____

3. It is <u>impossible</u> to draw a perfect picture of yourself!
   _____

4. My <u>bicycle</u> has a flat tire.
   _____

5. After only one year the garden was <u>overgrown</u>.
   _____

6. There was so much rain the river began to <u>overflow</u> its banks.
   _____

7. The storm passed <u>overnight</u> and the sun was shining this morning.
   _____

8. It is <u>impolite</u> to speak when your mouth is full of food.
   _____

9. I will <u>compose</u> a photo of different types of flowers.
   _____

10. Brandon flew <u>overseas</u> to see his aunt and uncle.
    _____

©2008 Plutarch Publications, Inc. PPI -1003

Name _____   Standard: Suffixes

A **SUFFIX** is a group of letters placed behind a word to change the meaning of that word. Each suffix has its own meaning. For example:

"ness" - state of being	Sick<u>ness</u> means "being sick or ill".
"en" - made of	Bright<u>en</u> means "made bright".
"ern" - of a direction	West<u>ern</u> means "part of the west".
"s" - more than one	Closet<u>s</u> means "more than one closet".

Read each sentence then write the meaning of the underlined word on the blank below.

1. When Kate's dog was lost, she was filled with <u>sadness</u>.
   _____

2. Mike found <u>fossils</u> of bird bones when he dug the hole in the yard.
   _____

3. Please <u>darken</u> the room so that we can watch the movie.
   _____

4. How many <u>pumpkins</u> do I need to make a pie?
   _____

5. Carrie is sweet and has <u>goodness</u> in her heart.
   _____

6. My classroom has seven <u>computers</u> for the students to use.
   _____

7. Louisiana is a <u>southern</u> state.
   _____

8. The glue must <u>harden</u> before we can use the broken cup again.
   _____

9. The sun rises in the <u>eastern</u> sky every morning.
   _____

10. There are some loose <u>threads</u> hanging from your sleeve.
    _____

Name _____   Standard: Suffixes

A **SUFFIX** is a group of letters placed behind a word to change the meaning of that word. Each suffix has its own meaning. For example:

"ful" - full of	Cheer<u>ful</u> means "full of cheer".
"less" - without	Care<u>less</u> means "without care".
"ly" - in what manner	Excited<u>ly</u> means "in an excited way".
"ous" - full of	Vari<u>ous</u> means "full of variety".

Read each sentence then write the meaning of the underlined word on the blank below.

1. The dog was <u>fearless</u> as he faced the raccoon.
   _____

2. It is <u>helpful</u> to have more than one pencil during a test.
   _____

3. Mrs. Green <u>nicely</u> offered us a piece of pie!
   _____

4. That artwork is <u>colorful</u> and interesting!
   _____

5. Dean <u>politely</u> asked if he could have another cookie.
   _____

6. The <u>dangerous</u> road had many curves and steep hills.
   _____

7. Greg was <u>hopeful</u> that he made the football team.
   _____

8. Watching those dark clouds over the lake makes me <u>nervous</u>.
   _____

9. The old newspapers were <u>worthless</u> so no one wanted them.
   _____

10. <u>Slowly</u> open your eyes so the bright sun doesn't hurt them.
    _____

Name _____   Standard: Suffixes

A **SUFFIX** is a group of letters placed behind a word to change the meaning of that word. Each suffix has its own meaning. For example:

"ship" - state or quality	Hard<u>ship</u> means "in a state of hard times".
"able" - worth or ability	Love<u>able</u> means "worth loving".
"like" - relating to	Home<u>like</u> means "relating to home or like home".
"er" - a person who	Explor<u>er</u> means "a person who explores".

Read each sentence then write the meaning of the underlined word on the blank below.

1. Our <u>friendship</u> will last for many years.

   _____

2. Mr. Wilder becomes <u>childlike</u> when he goes to a circus!

   _____

3. Jose is the <u>pitcher</u> for our baseball team.

   _____

4. This bed is so <u>comfortable</u> I overslept this morning!

   _____

5. We took <u>ownership</u> when we bought that car.

   _____

6. Gustav is a <u>dependable</u> worker.

   _____

7. That child <u>performer</u> can sing and dance very well.

   _____

8. The problem is <u>solvable</u> if we put our heads together and think.

   _____

9. The <u>traveler</u> drove through five states to visit his friend.

   _____

10. Can you believe how <u>lifelike</u> those silk flowers look?

    _____

©2008 Plutarch Publications, Inc. PPI -1003

Name _____   Standard: Figurative Language

> **FIGURATIVE LANGUAGE** is a colorful way to express an idea by drawing a picture with words and giving us a new way to see something. For example: "It is raining cats and dogs!"
> This does not mean that cats and dogs are falling from the sky. It makes an image exaggerating the amount of rain that is falling.

Each sentence below uses figurative language. Circle the choice that tells what the sentence really means.

1. Gretchen stood as still as a statue.

   Gretchen was frozen in ice.   **Gretchen was asleep.**

   Gretchen was standing very still.

2. Mr. Smith roared when the baseball broke his window.

   Mr. Smith was a lion.   **Mr. Smith yelled.**

   Mr. Smith was very sad.

3. Rosemary has cheeks like roses!

   Rosemary's cheeks are red.   **Rosemary smells good.**

   Rosemary has big cheeks.

4. My head is pounding like a bass drum.

   I am sick to my stomach.   **I have a bad headache.**

   I like to listen to music.

5. That basketball player is a skyscraper!

   The basketball player is quiet.   **The basketball player is tall.**

   The basketball player lives in the city.

6. Dan's house is like an oven today.

   Dan's house is hot.   **Dan is baking cookies.**

   Dan lives in the desert.

Name _____   Standard: Figurative Language

> **FIGURATIVE LANGUAGE** is a colorful way to express an idea by drawing a picture with words and giving us a new way to see something. For example: "Patty is as quiet as a mouse."
> This does not mean that Patty cannot talk or make noise. It makes an image exaggerating how quiet Patty is.

Each sentence below uses figurative language. Circle the choice that tells what the sentence really means

1. Mitchell piled his ice cream a mile high!

   Mitchell took a lot of ice cream.   **The ice cream was cold.**

   Mitchell was in an airplane.

2. Kristie strained her brain studying for the big test.

   Kristie had a headache.   **Kristie studied hard.**

   Kristie could not study.

3. This day has been a million years long!

   The day went by quickly.   **The day was over.**

   It was a long day.

4. Sandy's hands are like ice cubes.

   Sandy has cold hands.   **Sandy is standing in snow.**

   Sandy's hands are in her pockets.

5. The baby slept like a rock after playtime.

   The baby was snoring.   **The baby cried.**

   The baby was tired and slept well.

6. Nancy's hair is like velvet.

   Nancy's hair is tangled.   **Nancy's hair is soft.**

   Nancy has short curly hair.

©2008 Plutarch Publications, Inc. PPI-1003

Name _____   Standard: Context Clues

Put an **X** in the box beside the word that best completes each sentence.

1. Boil water in the _____ for tea.
   ☐ kiss   ☐ kettle   ☐ key

2. The workman wears a _____ to protect his head.
   ☐ helmet   ☐ hospital   ☐ hunter

3. The _____ wanted to buy a loaf of bread.
   ☐ churn   ☐ capture   ☐ customer

4. The _____ child was afraid of everything.
   ☐ treasure   ☐ tennis   ☐ timid

5. Is it time to _____ your birthday?
   ☐ clatter   ☐ celebrate   ☐ command

6. The warm sun and cool breeze make this a _____ day.
   ☐ pleasant   ☐ pebble   ☐ package

7. You must come in through the _____, not the exit.
   ☐ expert   ☐ emergency   ☐ entrance

8. King Roy had a green _____ in his crown.
   ☐ jewel   ☐ jelly   ☐ jaw

9. Does Randy know how to _____ that machine?
   ☐ object   ☐ operate   ☐ occur

10. Marcy _____ chewing gum.
    ☐ quiet   ☐ quarter   ☐ quit

©2008 Plutarch Publications, Inc. PPI -1003

Name _____   Standard: Context Clues

Put an **X** in the box beside the word that best completes each sentence.

1. We will go on an _____ in the jungle!		
☐ **address**	☐ **adventure**	☐ **admire**
2. The lion had a _____ growl!		
☐ **flame**	☐ **fierce**	☐ **fever**
3. There is a flower box on the window _____.		
☐ **listener**	☐ **lawn**	☐ **ledge**
4. The _____ train arrived two hours early!		
☐ **rapid**	☐ **remain**	☐ **route**
5. Wendy felt _____ as she waited for the principal.		
☐ **anxious**	☐ **accept**	☐ **approach**
6. Do not worry about the _____ until it gets here!		
☐ **forty**	☐ **further**	☐ **future**
7. Smog and smoke are kinds of _____.		
☐ **polish**	☐ **pollution**	☐ **precious**
8. The pinwheel began to _____ in colorful circles.		
☐ **waste**	☐ **whirl**	☐ **wrinkle**
9. Mack was _____ to go play at the beach.		
☐ **entire**	☐ **eager**	☐ **excuse**
10. Study hard and you will _____ your grades!		
☐ **improve**	☐ **immediate**	☐ **insist**

©2008 Plutarch Publications, Inc. PPI-1003

Name _____   Standard: Context Clues

Put an **X** in the box beside the word that best completes each sentence.

1. Be sure to _____ those dirty dishes!
   ☐ sharpen   ☐ slippery   ☐ scrub

2. My pencil is very _____ , just like yours.
   ☐ otherwise   ☐ ordinary   ☐ offer

3. Watch the speed _____ and go slowly here.
   ☐ laundry   ☐ limit   ☐ liquid

4. Don't _____ about having to clean your room!
   ☐ grind   ☐ gentle   ☐ grumble

5. That _____ puppy tore the newspaper.
   ☐ naughty   ☐ needle   ☐ national

6. We went to the _____ to see that new movie.
   ☐ theater   ☐ traffic   ☐ tunnel

7. The explorers went on a _____ to the North Pole.
   ☐ jerk   ☐ journey   ☐ judge

8. Would you like to _____ on some popcorn?
   ☐ material   ☐ motion   ☐ munch

9. Did you _____ your present yet?
   ☐ unwrap   ☐ usual   ☐ underneath

10. _____ the secret message after you read it!
    ☐ Skunk   ☐ Shred   ☐ Safety

©2008 Plutarch Publications, Inc. PPI -1003

Name _____   Standard: Context Clues

Put an **X** in the box beside the word that best completes each sentence.

1. The firemen will _____ the cat in the tree.
   ☐ **recipe**   ☐ **rocket**   ☐ **rescue**

2. I can always _____ on my best friend!
   ☐ **danger**   ☐ **depend**   ☐ **drawn**

3. Alice likes to _____ at the flowers in the garden.
   ☐ **gaze**   ☐ **graceful**   ☐ **glitter**

4. Put a _____ of sticks on the campfire.
   ☐ **biscuit**   ☐ **bounce**   ☐ **bundle**

5. Preston will _____ the treehouse by himself!
   ☐ **delicate**   ☐ **design**   ☐ **droop**

6. Did I _____ that I am very hungry?
   ☐ **mention**   ☐ **magical**   ☐ **memory**

7. In the fall, we _____ the ripe crops.
   ☐ **harbor**   ☐ **harvest**   ☐ **hatch**

8. Piper will go to the _____ with her parents.
   ☐ **banquet**   ☐ **beard**   ☐ **burst**

9. Can you _____ an enormous hill of jelly beans?
   ☐ **intelligent**   ☐ **impatient**   ☐ **imagine**

10. The rabbit began to _____ on the tender lettuce.
    ☐ **nonsense**   ☐ **narrow**   ☐ **nibble**

©2008 Plutarch Publications, Inc. PPI -1003

Name _____   Standard: Sequence of Events

Sequence of Events is the order in which things happen. Signal words like first, second, then, next, after, and finally help show the order of events. Read the stories then number the events in the correct sequence.

I am excited! This year at school I have a locker with a combination lock. First I have to spin the dial three times to the left. Next I turn right and point the arrow to the number 33. After that, I turn the dial left one full turn and stop on the number 41. I then turn the dial right and stop at the number 57. The next thing I do is pull on the lock and it opens. Finally, I pull up on the handle and open my locker. I can keep my coat and books in the locker instead of in my desk!

Open the lock:

_____ Turn right to number 33.

_____ Turn right to number 57.

_____ Pull up on the handle.

_____ Open my locker.

_____ Spin three times to the left.

_____ Stop on the number 41.

_____ Turn left one full turn.

_____ Pull to open the lock.

Make a pizza:

_____ Get out all the ingredients.

_____ Spread on the sauce.

_____ Add cheese.

_____ Eat the pizza.

_____ Add pepperoni.

_____ Let cool for one minute.

_____ Cook for two minutes

_____ Put the muffin on a plate.

Darren's favorite snack is pizza that he makes himself. The first thing he does is set all the ingredients on the kitchen counter. Next he puts an English muffin on a paper plate. He spreads the muffin with tomato sauce. After that he puts on pepperoni and then cheese. Darren puts the pizza in the microwave for two minutes. He takes the pizza out of the microwave and lets it cool for one minute. He pours a glass of milk. At last he can take a big bite of the home-made pizza!

Name _____   Standard: Sequence of Events

Sequence of Events is the order in which things happen. Signal words like first, second, then, next, after, and finally help show the order of events. Read the stories then number the events in the correct sequence.

To get the best grades and learn well, you should prepare a place to study. First, find a table that you can use. Clear off a spot for your books and paper. Make sure there is a lamp or light so you can see to read. Put your books on the table. Set out your paper and pencil to take notes. Pull up a comfortable chair. Begin to read and take notes. Be sure to take a break about every twenty minutes so you don't get too tired. Study for an hour or two. Good luck on your tests!

Ready for homework:

_____ Set your books on the table.

_____ Read and take notes.

_____ Put out paper and pencils.

_____ Take a break.

_____ Turn on a lamp or light.

_____ Clear off a spot on the table.

_____ Find a table.

_____ Get a comfortable chair.

Set the table:

_____ Forks go on each napkin.

_____ Put the napkins on the left.

_____ Glasses go above the forks.

_____ Spoons go next to the knives.

_____ Set the plates on the table.

_____ Fold the napkins.

_____ Knives are set to the right.

_____ Set flowers on the table.

Josie helps her mother by setting the table for dinner every night. First, Josie sets out the plates. She folds napkins then sets them to the left of each plate. Josie puts a fork on each napkin. Then she puts a bread knife on the right side of every plate. After that she puts a spoon next to each knife. When those things are done, Josie places a glass above the forks at each place setting. The last thing Josie does is set a vase of flowers in the middle of the table.

©2008 Plutarch Publications, Inc. PPI -1003

Name _____   Standard: Referents

> **REFERENTS** are words that take the place of a word so you don't have to repeat it many times. *She, it, they, he, a few, some,* and *we* are some of the referents we use. For example:
> Betty is running for class president. <u>She</u> wants to win the race!
> The word "She" refers to Betty without having to name her again.

Read the sentences below. Circle the word in the second sentence that stands for the underlined word or words in the first sentence.

1. <u>The people in my family</u> have many talents. They are artists!

2. <u>My mother</u> paints. She likes to paint portraits of people.

3. Mother paints with <u>watercolors</u>. They are easy to use and look nice.

4. <u>Grandpa</u> works with wood. He carves things out of sticks.

5. He has entered <u>his carvings</u> in contests. They often win prizes.

6. Designing gardens is what my <u>father</u> does. He likes working outdoors.

7. Father puts many <u>roses</u> in his gardens. He thinks they are beautiful.

8. <u>Grandma</u> is a florist. She arranges flowers and delivers them to customers.

9. Sometimes Grandma uses flowers from <u>Father's</u> gardens. She thinks his flowers are very colorful and nice.

10. My sister, <u>Katie</u>, is a dancer. Her class performs once a month.

11. They dance at the <u>theater</u> in town. It has an enormous stage.

12. <u>My whole family</u> goes to watch. We clap for Katie when the show is over.

13. <u>My talent</u> is very unusual. It takes a lot of patience and love.

14. My talent is cooking delicious <u>meals</u>. Everyone likes eating them!

©2008 Plutarch Publications, Inc. PPI-1003

Name _____

Standard: Referents

> **REFERENTS** are words that take the place of a word so you don't have to repeat it many times. *She, it, they, he, a few, some,* and *we* are some of the referents we use. For example:
>   The cat is sleeping in the basket. He likes to sleep there.
> The word "there" refers to "in the basket", the place where the cat sleeps.

Read each pair of sentences. On the line, write the word or words that refer to the underlined word.

1. Jack and Jake had an adventure today. <u>They</u> went on a hike to the lake in the park.
    They _____

2. The boys packed a picnic lunch. <u>They</u> rode bicycles all the way to the lake.
    They _____

3. When they got to the lake, Jack wanted to take a swim. The water was a little cold, but <u>he</u> wanted to jump in right away.
    He _____

4. Jake saw a boat in some bushes near the water. He thought <u>it</u> looked a little old, but strong enough to stay afloat.
    it _____

5. Jack wasn't sure that the boat was safe. <u>He</u> said the boards looked a little weak.
    He _____

6. Jack and Jake put the boat into the shallow water and got in. <u>The two of them</u> waited for a few minutes.
    The two of them _____

7. The boat began to fill up with water. Before long, <u>it</u> was up to the boy's ankles.
    it _____

8. Jake jumped out and dragged the boat back to shore. The boys agreed <u>it</u> was not safe enough to take for a ride across the lake!
    it _____

Name _____   Standard: Compare/Contrast

We **compare** and **contrast** things to find out
how they are **alike** and how they are **different**.

 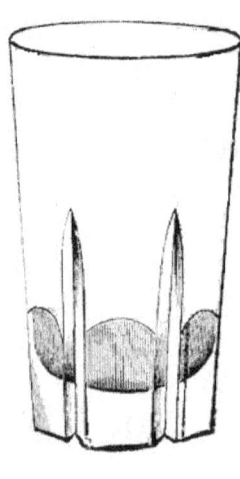

cup   glass

Read each statement below. If the statement describes the cup, write
C on the line. If the statement describes the glass, write **G** on the line. If
the statement describes both items, write **B** on the line.

_____ 1. I have a handle.
_____ 2. I am taller.
_____ 3. You can put liquid in me.
_____ 4. You can drink from me.
_____ 5. I am found in the kitchen.
_____ 6. You often put cold water or milk in me.
_____ 7. I am usually used for hot liquid.
_____ 8. I have a saucer
_____ 9. I have a lip or rim around my top.
_____ 10. I look like half of a ball.
_____ 11. I am taller than I am wide.
_____ 12. I am shorter.
_____ 13. From the top view I look round.
_____ 14. Adults use me for coffee or tea.
_____ 15. I can be cleaned in the dishwasher.

Name _____   Standard: Compare/Contrast

We **compare** and **contrast** things to find out
how they are **alike** and how they are **different**.

nickel

dime

Read each statement below. If the statement describes the nickel, write **N** on the line. If the statement describes the dime, write **D** on the line. If the statement describes both items, write **B** on the line.

_____ 1. I am a coin.
_____ 2. You can buy things with me.
_____ 3. I am worth more money than the other coin.
_____ 4. I have a "head" and a "tail".
_____ 5. My President is facing right.
_____ 6. I have a larger size than the other coin.
_____ 7. I am worth five pennies.
_____ 8. My President is facing left.
_____ 9. I am worth ten pennies.
_____ 10. I am round.
_____ 11. I am flat.
_____ 12. I have a smaller size than the other coin.
_____ 13. I have a date stamped on me.
_____ 14. People use me.
_____ 15. I am made of metal.

Name _____   Standard: Compare/Contrast

We **compare** and **contrast** things to find out
how they are **alike** and how they are **different**.

corn

watermelon

Read each statement below. If the statement describes the corn, write **C** on the line. If the statement describes the watermelon, write **S** on the line. If the statement describes both items, write **B** on the line.

_____ 1. I am round and red inside.
_____ 2. People eat me.
_____ 3. I have a papery husk covering my yellow inside.
_____ 4. I have a green covering.
_____ 5. I am wet and juicy.
_____ 6. Many people like to spit my seeds.
_____ 7. I have yellow kernels.
_____ 8. I am a vegetable.
_____ 9. I can be squeezed and made into a tasty breakfast drink.
_____ 10. I grow on tall stalks.
_____ 11. I am delicious.
_____ 12. You should cook me before I am eaten.
_____ 13. I am in the fruit family.
_____ 14. I come from a plant.
_____ 15. I am served hot.

©2008 Plutarch Publications, Inc. PPI -1003

Name _____   Standard: Cause and Effect

CAUSE is something that happens and **EFFECT** is the result. For example:

<u>Brian was hungry</u>, (so Mara made him a turkey sandwich.)

The event that happened, or CAUSE, was that Brian was hungry. The result, or EFFECT, was that Mara made a sandwich.

In each sentence below, underline the cause and circle the effect.

1. Casey didn't have a book to read, so he went to the library.

2. He had to wait outside for ten minutes because the library wasn't open yet.

3. The librarian opened the door because she arrived with the key.

4. She had several books in her arms so Casey held the door for her.

5. The librarian smiled and thanked him because he was so polite.

6. Casey didn't know where begin looking so he asked for some help.

7. Because he didn't know what kind of book to read, the librarian asked if he liked fiction or nonfiction better.

8. Casey usually read nonfiction, so he told the librarian he liked history books about inventions.

9. The librarian smiled because she knew just where to look.

10. The librarian led him to the shelves with books about inventions, and Casey was excited to have so many choices!

11. Because Casey looked at all the books, he found just the one he wanted.

12. Casey had found just the right book which pleased the librarian.

©2008 PLUTARCH PUBLICATIONS, Inc. PPI -1003

Name _____   Standard: Cause and Effect

CAUSE is something that happens and **EFFECT** is the result. For example:
(The carpet was wet) because Liam spilled his glass of juice.
The event that happened, or CAUSE, was that Liam spilled juice.
The result, or EFFECT, was that the carpet was wet.

In each sentence below, underline the cause and circle the effect.

1. Flashy, a little fish, was sad because he had no one to play with.

2. Because the water was sunny and bright, it looked like a great day to play and have a grand adventure!

3. Flashy couldn't see any friends outside, so he went to find them.

4. Finny's house was dark, so Flashy knew no one was home.

5. Bubble's Mother came to the door when Flashy knocked.

6. She said Bubbles wasn't feeling well so she couldn't come out to play.

7. Because he was gone to his swimming lessons, Flashy's friend Octy couldn't play either.

8. Flashy was sad because his friends could not play with him.

9. He swam in slow circles because he did not know what else to do.

10. Flashy looked down at the sand beneath him, and that made him notice his shadow below.

11. Since there was no one else around, Flashy decided to play tag with his own shadow!

12. Flashy was finally happy because the sun had given him a friend!

©2008 Plutarch Publications, Inc. PPI-1003

Name _____   Standard: Conclude/Predict

> Sometimes the events in a story can give clues as to what is going to happen. You can use those clues to **PREDICT,** or tell what might happen next.

Read each paragraph below and predict what will probably happen next. Circle your answer.

1. Levi and Josh were playing ball. Levi said he could throw the ball farther than Josh. Josh said that he could throw the ball farther. What will probably happen?

   A. The boys will go home and watch television.

   B. The boys will take turns trying to throw the ball as far as they can.

   C. The boys will play a game of baseball.

2. Marge was drinking grape juice in the living room where she wasn't supposed to eat or drink. Marge spilled her glass of juice on the carpet. It left a big purple stain. What will probably happen?

   A. Marge's parents will bring her a present.

   B. The stain will disappear by itself.

   C. Marge's parents will be upset with her.

3. Dark clouds were gathering overhead. It began to thunder and the wind started to blow. Lightning flashed across the sky! What will probably happen?

   A. It will rain.

   B. It will snow.

   C. A rainbow will appear.

4. Craig could hear his mother in the kitchen. He sniffed deeply as good smells drifted from the kitchen. Craig set plates, glasses, and napkins on the table. What will probably happen?

   A. The family will watch a movie.

   B. The family will sit down to eat.

   C. Craig will fall asleep on the couch.

©2008 Plutarch Publications, Inc. PPI-1003

Name _____   Standard: Conclude/Predict

> Often, you can use your own experiences to understand even more than the author tells you. That is called **DRAWING CONCLUSIONS**.

Read each paragraph below and answer the question by DRAWING A CONCLUSION. Circle your answer.

1. Amy stood in her backyard with the leash in her hand. She looked everywhere, but she could not find her dog. She called "Sparky! Come here, Sparky!" but there was no answer. How is Amy feeling?

    A. Amy is happy that she can't find her dog.
    B. Amy is worried that the dog is lost.
    C. Amy is sleepy.

2. Marcus yawned and stretched, then pushed back the blanket. The smell of pancakes and bacon drifted in from the kitchen. Marcus jumped out of bed. What time of day is it?

    A. It is morning.
    B. It is late at night and time to go to bed.
    C. It is after school.

3. Randy rubbed his cold hands together and wished he had brought his gloves. His boots and jacket were warm, but his hood was not snug enough to cover his ears. What is the weather like?

    A. It is raining.
    B. It is warm and breezy.
    C. It is cold and maybe snowing.

4. Emily and Chris each got a tray and stood in line. As they moved forward, Emily took a salad but Chris chose a bowl of peaches. They both took the ham and mashed potatoes. Where are they?

    A. Emily and Chris are at the movie theater.
    B. Emily and Chris are in the lunch line at school.
    C. Emily and Chris are having a picnic in the park.

Name _____   Standard: Author's Purpose

Authors have a **PURPOSE**, or reason, for the things they write. One purpose is to tell facts or true stories. Another purpose is to amuse or entertain the reader.

Tell the PURPOSE for each type of written work listed. Write **F** on the line if the purpose is to give facts or information. Write **A** if the purpose is to entertain.

_____ 1. newspaper story about the mayor

_____ 2. book of jokes

_____ 3. Science book

_____ 4. comic strip in the newspaper

_____ 5. book of poems

_____ 6. nursery rhymes

_____ 7. dictionary

_____ 8. comic book

_____ 9. story about a rabbit that talks

_____ 10. story about Abraham Lincoln

_____ 11. mystery story

_____ 12. book about planets and stars

_____ 13. Math book

_____ 14. fashion magazine

_____ 15. book about your state

_____ 16. fairy tales

_____ 17. book about whales and sharks

_____ 18. an article about the President

_____ 19. cook book

_____ 20. guide for learning about computers

©2008 Plutarch Publications, Inc. PPI -1003

Name _____   Standard: Genre

> **Genre** is the style in which a story is written. Three types of genre are:
> **Fantasy** - characters can do things they never could in the real world
> **Biography** - the life story about a real person
> **Fairy Tale** - imaginary creatures and magic with a happy ending

Read the statements below. On the line write **F** if the book is fantasy, **B** if it is a biography, and **FT** if it is a fairy tale.

_____ 1. *Amanda Pig and Her Big Brother Oliver,* by Jean Van Leeuwen, is a story about a pig named Oliver and his troubles with his little sister, Amanda, who always follows him around.

_____ 2. *Wanted Dead or Alive: the True Story of Harriet Tubman,* by Ann Mcgovern, tells the story of a female slave who escapes to freedom. Then she helps other slaves become free.

_____ 3. *Rapunzel,* by Bernice Chardiet, is the story of a princess with long hair who is put under a magic spell by a wicked witch. The girl is locked in a tower and rescued by a prince.

_____ 4. *Day of the Dragon King,* by Mary Pope Osborne, is an exciting story about two children who have a treehouse that takes them back in time. They go back to ancient China on a mission to find a book and save the library.

_____ 5. *Louisa May Alcott: Young Novelist,* by Beatrice Gormley, is the story of Louisa's childhood. Her family was poor and she almost died, but she grew up to become a famous author.

_____ 6. *Rumpelstiltskin,* by the brothers Grimm, is the story of an odd looking little man who saves a princess by spinning hay into gold. The princess has to give the man her first child unless she can guess his name.

Name _____   Standard: Narrative Comprehension

My name is Matt. I live in a small town in **Iowa**, a state in the north. There are thirty-two people in the **entire**, or whole, third grade at school! There are many good things about having such a small class. I know everyone and they all know me. I can walk all the way across town in less than fifteen minutes, so getting around is easy. Living in a small town is like having one big family. We all watch out for each other and help each other. There are some problems with living in a small town. We only have one grocery store, bank, restaurant and gas station. There is no place to buy clothes so we must drive to a city nearby for that kind of shopping or to go to a movie. But, living in a small town makes me feel safe and comfortable. I wouldn't want to live anywhere else!

1. What is the name of the boy in the story? _____
2. In which state does he live? _____

Name three things the boy likes about living in a small town.

3. _____
4. _____
5. _____

6. What is not so good about living in a small town?

_____
_____

7. What does the word "entire" mean?
   A. tired   B. whole   C. small

8. What would be a good title for this story?
   A. A Boy Named Matt
   B. Living in a Small Town
   C. City Life

 **Find it:** Find Iowa on a map of the United States.

 **Imagine it:** What is it like living in a small town?

Name _____   Standard: Narrative Comprehension

 Isabela lives with her grandmother and grandfather in the western state of **Arizona**. They live in a town near the **desert**, a warm dry area with lots of sand. Isabela and her grandmother enjoy having picnics in the desert. They like to pack a lunch and ride their horses into the desert. They look at the different **cacti**, or plants that grow well in the desert because they don't need much water. The tall **saguaro** cactus looks like it has many branches reaching up into the wide blue sky! Isabela and grandmother often sit in the shade of that large plant when they stop for lunch. Isabela loves living near the desert, even though the weather is hot and dry. At night it cools down and every star shines brightly in the dark desert sky.

1. What is the name of the girl in the story? _____
2. In which state does she live? _____

   Name three things the story tells you about the desert.

3. _____
4. _____
5. _____
6. What is a "saguaro"?
   _____
   _____

7. What is a "desert"?
   A. a sweet treat   B. saguaro   C. a warm dry land
8. What would be a good title for this story?
   A. Isabela and the Horses
   B. Grandmother Makes a Picnic
   C. Fun In The Desert

 **Find it:** Find Arizona on a map of the United States.   **Compare it:** How are the desert and your town alike?

©2008 Plutarch Publications, Inc. PPI-1003

Name _____ Standard: Narrative Comprehension

Ben and his friends are going swimming today. They live in **Florida** near the ocean and like to spend their summer days at the beach. Ben will bring his swim mask and **snorkel**, a tube that lets him breathe underwater. Randy and Joe will bring their snorkels, too. The boys will swim in the **shallow** water, where it is not deep, and look at all the plants and animals. Sometimes they will see schools of brightly colored fish. Other times they find small animals among the long seaweed that grows there. When they are tired of swimming, they like to explore along the beach. They find shells and smooth bits of wood that have washed up on the shore. The three boys end the day by building a giant sandcastle!

1. Who is the main character in this story? _____
2. In which state does he live? _____

Name three things the boys can do at the beach.

3. _____
4. _____
5. _____

6. What is a "snorkel"?
   _____
   _____

7. What does the word "shallow" mean?
   A. not deep   B. deep   C. colorful fish

8. What would be a good title for this story?
   A. A Day at the Beach
   B. Ben Goes Swimming
   C. How to Build a Sandcastle

 **Find it:** Find Florida on a map of the United States.

 **Think about it:** What do you like to do at the beach?

©2008 Plutarch Publications, Inc. PPI-1003

Name _____   Standard: Narrative Comprehension

Winona lives in the Black Hills of **South Dakota**. The hills are covered with tall dark pine trees, and from far away that makes the hills look black! Winona's best friend is Wapi, her **cousin** (the child her aunt and uncle). Winona and Wapi often like to hike in the woods near their home. They walk quietly so they don't scare away the animals that live there. Winona takes a camera and gets a picture of the animals they find. Wapi brings a notebook and pencil so he can takes notes to remember where they saw each animal. When they get home, Winona and Wapi take out their photo album and add the new pictures and notes. They have pictures of deer, mountain goats, a gopher, and even a **bison** (an animal that looks like a buffalo).

1. Who is the main character in this story? _____
2. In which state does she live? _____

   Name three animals pictured in the photo album.

3. _____
4. _____
5. _____

6. What is a "bison"?
   _____
   _____

7. What word means "an uncle or aunt's child"?
   A. cousin   B. camera   C. gopher

8. What would be a good title for this story?
   A. The Black Hills
   B. Winona's Cousin
   C. Winona and Wapi Take Animal Photos

 **Find it:** Find South Dakota on a map of the United States.

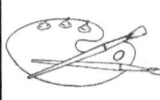 **Draw it:** Draw a picture of an animal you might see in your state.

©2008 Plutarch Publications, Inc. PPI-1003

Name _____ Standard: Narrative Comprehension

Vinnie lives in New York City, the largest city in the state of **New York**. The tall buildings called **skyscrapers** keep the streets in shade unless the sun is directly overhead at noontime! Vinnie and his friends go to a school in one of the tall buildings. It is fun to ride the elevator up to the twenty-second floor. When Vinnie looks out one window during class, he can see the city spread out for miles. From another window Vinnie can see the Hudson River with **New Jersey** on the other side. He can even see the Statue of Liberty in the bay! After school, Vinnie and his friends walk to their apartments. They like to stop and buy a hotdog or some roasted peanuts from the street **vendor**, a person who sells things from a cart. Sometimes they stop in a small park and feed the nuts to squirrels. On rainy days, the boys will share a taxi ride home!

1. Who is the main character in this story? _____
2. In which state does he live? _____

Name three things Vinnie can see from his classroom.

3. _____
4. _____
5. _____

6. What is a "vendor"?

_____
_____

7. What does the word "skyscraper" mean?
   A. tall buildings   B. twenty floors   C. directly

8. What would be a good title for this story?
   A. New York
   B. Vinnie Lives in New York City
   C. Vinnie and the Hotdog Man

 **Find it:** Find New York and New Jersey on a map of the United States.

 **Think about it:** If you could visit New York City, what would you most like to see?

©2008 Plutarch Publications, Inc. PPI-1003

Name _____   Standard: Narrative Comprehension

Susan lives on a farm in **Kansas**. Her grandpa bought the farm when he married grandma over forty years ago. Susan's father, George, was born and raised on that farm. Now Susan's family lives in that same house. **Acres**, or large fields, of land surround the house and each spring it is planted with wheat. They use enormous tractors to plow the land and plant the seeds. Every fall the wheat is harvested and sold. It is ground into flour that is used in bread, cake, cookies, pasta, and noodles. Some of the **grain**, or seeds from the plant, are used as food for cattle. The stems from the wheat can be dried to make **straw** used as bedding for the farm animals. Susan is proud because she knows that people all over the world need the wheat her family grows. Susan thinks it would be wonderful to own the farm someday and raise her own family there!

1. Who is the main character in this story? _____
2. In which state does he live? _____

Name three things that can be made from wheat.

3. _____
4. _____
5. _____

6. What is an "acre"?
_____
_____

7. In this story, what does the word "straw" mean?
   A. not worth much   B. a dried plant stem   C. a tube to drink from

8. What would be a good title for this story?
   A. Susan's Farm
   B. Planting Crops
   C. Kansas

 **Find it:** Find Kansas on a map of the United States.

 **Look for it:** What other food are made from wheat? Try to find at least five.

©2008 Plutarch Publications, Inc. PPI -1003

Name _____   Standard: Narrative Comprehension

Chelsea lives in **Maine**. Her home is near the beach on the Atlantic Ocean. The salty smell of the air and the sound of the waves roaring to the beach always make Chelsea smile. She can't imagine anywhere else she would rather live. Chelsea loves going to the beach in the evening when the tide is out and the water is low. She wears a jacket because the evening breeze can make her **shiver** with cold at times. Tonight Chelsea is wearing a pair of tall boots. She has a flashlight, **bucket** (pail), shovel, and a hand rake. Chelsea shines her light across the wet sand, looking for bubbles. When she sees one, she quickly digs a hole under the bubble. Chelsea squeals with delight when her work uncovers a bed of clams nestled in the sand. She scoops them out with the rake and puts them into her bucket. Now she can have baked clams for dinner!

1. Who is the main character in this story? _____
2. In which state does he live? _____

   Name three things Chelsea takes with her to the beach.
3. _____
4. _____
5. _____

6. What causes Chelsea to "shiver"?
   _____
   _____

7. What is another word for "bucket"?
   A. pail   B. clam   C. shiver

8. What would be a good title for this story?
   A. The Atlantic Coast
   B. A Delicious Dinner
   C. Digging for Clams

 **Find it:** Find Maine on a map of the United States.

 **Write about it:** What things in your neighborhood make it special in the evening?

Name _____   Standard: Narrative Comprehension

Clyde and his family live in the Blue Ridge Mountains of **Kentucky**. His father is a ranch hand for a huge horse farm. One night Clyde's father woke him and told him to get dressed. One of the **mares** (female horses) had just given birth to a new **foal**, or baby horse. Clyde was dressed and ready to go in just a few minutes. As Clyde and his dad drove up to the **stable**, or barn where the animals are kept, they could see the vet had already arrived. The stable was warm and Clyde could hear the other horses making soft noises as their sleep was disturbed by the visitors. When he looked into the stall, Clyde could see the baby horse next to its mother. The foal was already trying to stand up on its long, shaky legs. After three more tries, the foal got to its feet! In only a few more minutes it was able to walk a few feet to its mother. Clyde was sure he would never forget this night!

1. Who is the main character in this story? _____
2. In which state does he live? _____

   Tell three things Clyde saw after he went into the stable.

3. _____
4. _____
5. _____
6. What is a "stable"?
   _____
   _____

7. What does the word "mare" mean?
      A. soft noises   B. foal   C. female horse
8. What would be a good title for this story?
      A. A New Foal
      B. Clyde and His Father
      C. Clyde's Horses

 **Find it:** Find Kentucky on a map of the United States.

 **Look for it:** Read a book about horses. Find three facts you didn't know.

Name _____   Standard: Narrative Comprehension

It was an exciting day for Inola. She lived on the Nantahala River on the eastern **border**, or edge, of **North Carolina**. As Inola grew up, she spent many summer days splashing in the **shallow** (not very deep) water of the river near her home. She learned to fish in that river and enjoyed eating the rainbow trout that she caught. As she grew older, Inola learned to swim in the deeper water. Now she was ready for the best adventure of all. Inola was going on her first whitewater rafting trip! She had watched the big yellow rafts and listened to the people laugh and have a good time as they floated by. She knew that she would go over a few small waterfalls made by sudden drops in the river. She knew that many rafters tipped over or fell into the chilly water, but that didn't scare her. She was excited! Today it would be her turn, and she could hardly wait!

1. Who is the main character in this story? _____

2. In which state does he live? _____

Name three things Inola did in the river as she grew up.

3. _____

4. _____

5. _____

6. What is a "border"?

_____

_____

7. What does the word "shallow" mean?

   A. not deep   B. deep   C. colorful fish

8. What would be a good title for this story?

   A. Fishing in the River

   B. Inola's Special Day

   C. Rafting and Swimming

 **Find it:** Find North Carolina on a map of the United States.

 **Draw it:** What one thing would you like to do someday? Draw a picture of it.

©2008 Plutarch Publications, Inc. PPI-1003

Name _____ Standard: Expository Comprehension

Inventions

Early man did not have things like lights, boats, glass, or money. Everything we use each day was an **invention** (something made from an idea). We have socks because someone thought about covering their cold feet with a piece of cloth. They sewed the sock in the shape of a foot and it kept their toes toasty. An invention was born! Many inventions are things that were **necessary**, or needed, and people made them. Other inventions were wild ideas that few could even **imagine**, or see in their mind. For example, capturing sound and sending it through wires was an impossible idea until 1875 when Alexander Graham Bell found a way to do it. Today most of the people in the world have used a telephone, and many of us carry one right in our pocket! Not every idea will become an invention, but there could be no inventions without ideas!

Name seven inventions you use every day (not the ones in the story).

1. _____
2. _____
3. _____
4. _____
5. _____
6. _____
7. _____

8. What is another word for "necessary"?

    A. idea   B. needed   C. impossible

9. What does the word "imagine" mean?

_____

10. Who invented the telephone and in what year?

_____

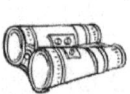

Think about it: Copy the list of inventions you named above. Why do you think each was necessary? What would life be like without each of them?

Name _____   Standard: Expository Comprehension

Up, Up, and Away!

The Aztecs were the first known people to use balloons. They cleaned bladders taken from cats, sewed them with a vegetable thread, and blew them into different shapes. Many cultures, such as the Eskimo and Indians, also played with bladder balloons. In 1783, two frenchmen made a 35 foot balloon of waxed paper and warmed the air in it, causing the balloon to rise. This was the invention of the "hot air" balloon. With the invention of rubber, balloons became easier to make. In 1824, rubber balloons were used in experiments with gases like **hydrogen**. These gases were lighter than air, allowing balloons to rise high into the sky without having to warm them. By 1889, people in the United States who enjoyed playing with these toys, could buy balloons for about four cents each. **Latex**, a type of stretchy rubber, was used in 1931.

1. What is the title of this story? _____
2. What is "hydrogen"? _____

Name three cultures that made bladder balloons.

3. _____
4. _____
5. _____

6. What product is a type of stretchy rubber?

    A. hydrogen   B. latex   C. waxed paper

7. What was used to sew bladder balloons? _____
8. In what year did balloons cost four cents? _____

The story lists four things balloons were made from. List three:

9. _____
10. _____
11. _____

Do it: Blow up a balloon and examine it. Can you make one of your own? Try different materials and see if you can make a balloon. What works? What doesn't work?

©2008 Plutarch Publications, Inc. PPI -1003

The Can Opener

The tin can, first used in 1810, was a good way to **preserve** food (keep it fresh). Cans were a good way to carry food for soldiers and travelers and they kept the food fresh for many months. Those cans were very thick and had to be opened with a hammer or the end of the soldier's rifle. This was messy and sometimes dangerous because of the sharp, ragged edges on the can. Soon cans were made thinner and were much easier to open. In 1858, Ezra Warner invented the first can opener. He got a **patent** for it, which is proof of legal ownership for an invention. His can opener had a sharp edge which was pushed into the can. The other end of the can opener, which looked like a hook, was then used to saw around the edge of the lid. In the 1870's, William Lyman designed a can opener with a cutting wheel, just like the ones we use today.

1. What is the title of this story? _____
2. What does the word "patent" mean? _____
_____

Name two ways that thick cans were opened.

4. _____
5. _____

6. What does the word "preserve" mean?
   A. keep safe   B. dangerous   C. ragged

7. What made cans easier to open? _____
8. Who invented the 1870 can opener? _____
9. Why were the first cans so difficult to open? _____
10. In your own words, explain how Ezra Warner's can opener worked.
_____
_____

Share it: Use the newspaper, magazines, and the computer to find different types of can openers. Make a poster that shows how they have changed over the years.

Name _____   Standard: Expository Comprehension

Wash Those Dishes!

The first machine invented to wash dishes was built in 1850. The wooden box splashed water on the dishes, but it didn't clean them well. A **wealthy** (rich) woman, Josephine Cochrane, waited for someone to invent a dishwasher that would do the job. No one did, so she decided to invent one herself! First, she designed wire racks to hold the dishes. Second, the racks were slipped inside **boiler**, or heater, with a water wheel. Third, the wheel shot hot, soapy water on the dishes. Josephine's dishwasher worked well, so she patented it. In 1893 she **displayed**, or showed, it to the public for the first time at the World's Fair and she won an award. Hotels and restaurants were very interested and the Cochrane Dishwasher was a hit. In the 1950's it became popular to have a dishwasher in the home, and today many homes have one.

1. What is the title of this story? _____
2. What does it mean to be "wealthy"? _____

List the three steps to using the Cochrane Dishwasher:

3. _____
4. _____
5. _____

6. What does it mean to "display" something?

    A. wash it   B. invent it   C. show it

7. What is a "boiler"? _____
8. In what year was the first dishwasher invented? _____

What two types of businesses were the first to use the dishwasher?

9. _____
10. _____

11. When did dishwashers become popular in homes? _____

Think about it: Which do you like best, washing dishes by hand or putting them in the dishwasher? What makes hand washing better? What makes using a dishwasher better?

©2008 Plutarch Publications, Inc. PPI-1003

Name _____ Standard: Expository Comprehension

Invented or Discovered?

Joshua Lionel Cowen, the inventor of the flashlight in 1989, owned a battery company. He invented the flashlight totally by **accident**, not on purpose! Joshua wanted a lamp to light up potted plants in his store. He **fashioned**, or made, a long metal tube and attached a small lightbulb. Batteries kept it lit for thirty days. He sold this invention in his battery store, and people found it much more useful as a portable light, one that could be carried anywhere without wires attached. Conrad Hubert, a sales person at the store, gave the flashlight its name. The flashlight became very popular and soon Mr. Cowen was very rich. In 1900, he wanted to advertise a sale item in his front window. He thought a tiny car that ran on a track might catch people's attention. The car didn't work well, so he made a tiny train instead. Not many people wanted the sale item, but everyone loved the train, so the Lionel Train Company was born. It still makes trains today!

1. What is the title of this story? _____
2. What is an "accident"? _____

Name three parts of the flashlight:

3. _____
4. _____
5. _____

6. The first toy train was invented for what use?

   A. a new toy   (B. a store display)   C. to light up plants

7. What was the first flashlight supposed to be? _____
8. In what year was the toy train invented? _____
9. Who gave the flashlight its name? _____
10. In your own words, tell how the toy train was invented:

    _____
    _____

Think about it: Can you remember a time when something you did by accident ended up being a good thing? Share your story with three other people and listen to their stories.

Name _____ Standard: Expository Comprehension

Cut the Grass

Yards with trimmed and tidy grass were first found in France in the 1700's. People liked the neat **lawns** and soon the idea spread to the rest of the world. The first "lawn mowers" were actually animals that **grazed**, or ate the grass during the day. That kept the grass short, but it wasn't even and the animals left the lawn messy. Tools like scissors and **sickles** (curved blades with handles) were used for many years, but they didn't cut evenly. In 1830, Edwin Budding put blades around a **cylinder**, or wide tube, and attached wheels and a long handle. Horses pulled the mower and the blades clipped the grass evenly. This worked well, but the horses had to wear leather booties so they didn't leave hoof prints on the lawn. In 1870, Elwood McGuire made a lawnmower that was light enough for humans to push. It left the lawn even and without footprints!

1. What is the title of this story? _____
2. What is a "sickle"? _____

The story tells three ways lawns have been cut. List them:

3. _____
4. _____
5. _____

6. What does the word "graze" mean?

    A. eat grass   B. tidy   C. cover with sugar

7. In what year was the horse-pulled mower invented? _____
8. In what year was the human push-mower invented? _____

List three reasons why animals were not good for mowing lawns:

9. _____
10. _____
11. _____

 Compare it: Find a picture of a human push mower used in the 1950's. Compare it to the lawnmower used today. How are they alike? How are they different?

©2008 Plutarch Publications, Inc. PPI -1003

Name _____   Standard: Expository Comprehension

Fasten Up

The very first paperclip was a ribbon that slid through two holes in the upper left corner of papers. The ribbon was tied, holding the papers together. The ribbon paperclip was used as early as the 1200's! Often the knot in the ribbon was **difficult** to untie, and had to be cut from the paper. People solved that problem by dipping the ribbons in wax, which made them stronger and easier to untie. That form of paper clip was used for almost 600 years. In 1899 a man from Norway invented the metal wire paperclip. His paperclips were small hoops in the shape of **double**-sided (two sided) triangles △ and rectangles ▭. Paper could be slipped between the two hoops, holding them together. A company in England designed the familiar oval shaped paperclip still widely used today.

1. What is the title of this story? _____
2. What does "double" mean? _____

The story tells of three shapes for the metal paperclip. Name them:

3. _____
4. _____
5. _____

6. What does the word "difficult" mean?

    A. hoop   B. tied   C. hard

7. Of what material was the first paperclip made ? _____
8. In what year was the metal paperclip invented? _____

List two reasons why the ribbon was not a good paperclip:

9. _____
10. _____
11. What made the ribbon work better? _____

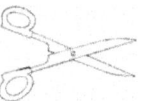

Make it: Can you invent a better paperclip? Use different materials to design a paperclip of your own. Be creative!

Name _____

Standard: Expository Comprehension

Would You Like a Sip?

Would you like some rye grass for your drink? Before straws were invented, people used dried rye grass (straw) because it formed a natural tube that could be used to remove liquid from a glass. In 1888, Marvin Stone wrapped paper strips into a **coil** (a set of loops) around a pencil and glued them together to make the first paper straw. The problem was that the paper became soggy and often **collapsed**, or flattened out, when used for just a few minutes. Marvin used a heavier paper dipped in a thin wax, and the straw was born! By 1906 the straw had become popular and machines were invented that could coil the paper and produce many straws in a short time. Plastic straws were invented in the 1960's and quickly replaced paper straws. Plastic stays dry and does not collapse easily, but plastic trash is harmful to the Earth. Today, some restaurants have gone back to paper straws to help save the Earth.

1. What is the title of this story? _____
2. What is a "coil"? _____

Name three types of straws talked about in the story:

3. _____

4. _____

5. _____

6. What does the word "collapse" mean?

    A. move liquid   B. flatten out   C. waxed paper

7. Who invented the paper straw? _____
8. In what year was the paper straw invented? _____
9. How did machines change the way straws were made?

_____

_____

10. When did plastic straws replace paper straws? _____

 **Find it:** Which is more popular where you live, plastic or paper straws? For one month, keep a list of the type of straws used in your favorite restaurants. Share your findings with others.

©2008 Plutarch Publications, Inc. PPI-1003

Name _____   Standard: Expository Comprehension

It's Raining

Umbrellas were used in China, Greece, and Egypt more than 4000 years ago! Those first umbrellas, called **parasols**, were made of paper and were used to shade people from the hot sun. The **Chinese** (people from China) were the first to make parasols **waterproof** by coating them with wax. That made the parasol useful when it rained because the water ran off instead of soaking into the paper. The waxy parasol was later renamed "umbrella", a Latin word that means "shade or shadow". Women in Europe started using umbrellas in the 1500's. Their umbrellas were made from wood or whalebone covered with an oily cloth. Fancy handles made of carved wood or ivory were added, and men began to carry them as well. In 1852, Samuel Fox made the first umbrella with metal "ribs" covered with a waterproof cloth. It was very much like the type of umbrella we still use today.

1. What is the title of this story? _____
2. What is a "parasol"? _____

Name three differences between the parasol and today's umbrella:

3. _____
4. _____
5. _____

6. What word means "treated to prevent from getting wet"?

    A. waterproof   B. shade   C. whalebone

7. When did Europeans start using umbrellas? _____
8. What did the Europeans add to umbrellas? _____

List two countries that were the first to invent parasols:

9. _____
10. _____

11. What does the word "umbrella" mean? _____

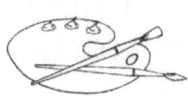
Draw it: Draw a picture of a rainy day and people using umbrellas. Find pictures of different umbrellas and glue them on paper to make a colorful collage.

Name _____   Standard: Maps/Charts

MAPS are useful tools that show streets, buildings, parks, and other places of interest. They also show distance and direction.

Use this map to answer the questions below.

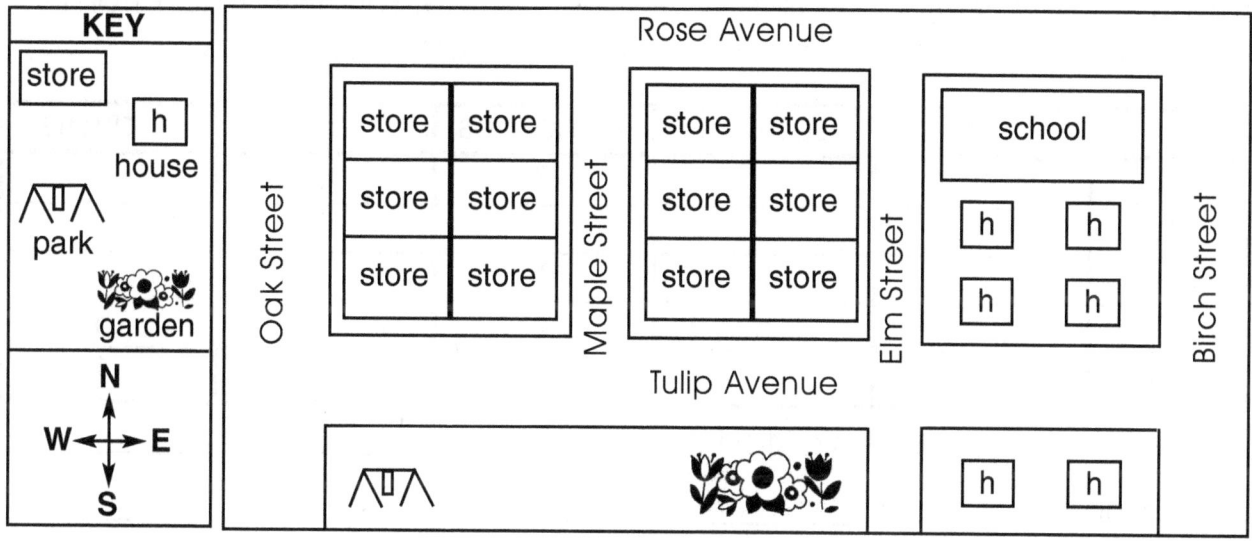

1. How many stores are shown on this map? _____
2. How many homes are shown on this map? _____
3. Where would you look to find out what /\⎕/\ is? _____
4. Is the school on the west or east side of the map? _____
5. What is found on the same block as the park? _____
6. The school is on which two streets?
    A. Tulip and Oak   B. Maple and Rose   C. Rose and Birch
7. Which street is further West, Maple or Elm? _____
8. The park and garden are both on what street? _____
9. Which avenue is further North, Tulip or Rose? _____
10. Are the houses on the East or West side of the map? _____
11. Are the houses North or South of the school? _____
12. What is directly West of the garden? _____

Name _____   Standard: Maps/Charts

> A **CHART** is a table that gives information in a list, making it easier to read and understand.

The Tyson family planted a vegetable garden. Each person kept a record of how many seeds they planted. Father made a chart from the information. Use this chart to answer the questions below.

	Corn	Lettuce	Tomatoes	Onions	Carrots
Jerry	3	1	7	1	5
Beth	5	0	2	0	3
Marvin	4	2	1	1	4
Mother	4	5	4	1	5
Father	8	4	4	3	4

1. How many people planted seeds? _____
2. Name the people: _____
   _____
3. Name the kinds of seeds that were planted: _____
   _____
4. Who planted the least tomatoes? _____
5. Jerry planted 7 seeds of which vegetable? _____
6. Which vegetable did Father plant most? _____
7. Which two vegetables do you think Beth does not like very much?
      A. lettuce & onions   B. corn & beans   C. lettuce & carrots
8. Who planted the most onions? _____
9. Who planted the least number of carrots? _____
10. Which two people each planted four corn seeds?
       A. Marvin & Father   B. Mother & Father   C. Mother & Marvin
11. Which vegetable had the least number of seeds planted in all?
       A. corn   B. onions   C. lettuce

©2008 Plutarch Publications, Inc. PPI-1003

Name _____   Standard: Maps/Charts

A **TIMELINE** is a chart that shows the order in which events happened.

Read Olive and Ryan's stories. Put the letter of each event on the blank under the timeline to show the proper order of their events.

Olive had a busy day last Saturday. She got up at 6:30 because there was much to do. She fixed pancakes for the family breakfast and they ate at 7:00. By 7:30 Olive finished washing and drying the dishes. At 8:00, Olive put on her work clothes and helped mother dust the house. At 8:30 she went outside and helped Father weed the garden. They finished at 9:00 and Olive sat on the swing to take a short rest.

A. finished dishes
B. put on work clothes
C. got out of bed
D. sat down to rest
E. weeded the garden
F. ate breakfast

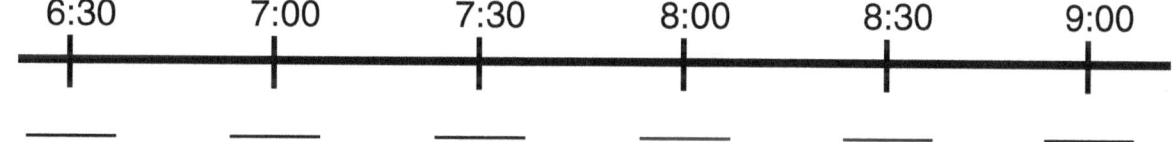

6:30   7:00   7:30   8:00   8:30   9:00

____   ____   ____   ____   ____   ____

Ryan wrote a story telling about the important things that happened in his life. He got his first puppy when he was three years old. Ryan started school at five years old. When he was only one, Ryan took his first ride in an airplane. His favorite birthday was at the zoo when he turned six. His sister, Ruth, was born when he was two. Best of all, Ryan went to Colorado and saw the Grand Canyon when he was four.

A. got a puppy
B. started school
C. first ride in an airplane
D. birthday party at the zoo
E. sister was born
F. took a trip to the Grand Canyon

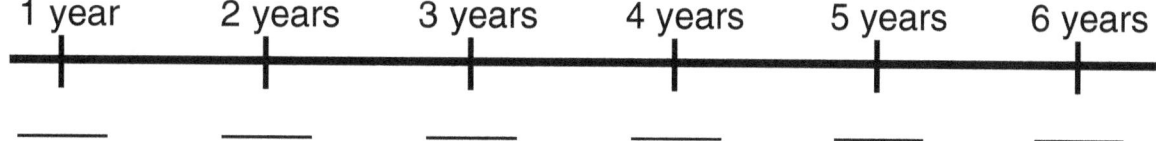

1 year   2 years   3 years   4 years   5 years   6 years

____   ____   ____   ____   ____   ____

©2008 Plutarch Publications, Inc. PPI-1003

Name _____   Standard: Forms/Signs

Signs are an important part of our lives. They give us information, keep us safe, and help us find places. Below are six signs we see every day.

Read each sentence below. Decide which of the above signs you might find in that situation. Write the letter of that sign on the blank.

_____ 1. You are on a busy street near a school. Children are waiting at the corner. A crossing guard is helping them cross the street to get to school. Which sign would you see?

_____ 2. You are in a restaurant and you have had two glasses of water. You need to go to the restroom. Which sign would you look for?

_____ 3. You are in a car going to the mall on the other side of the city. You see train tracks crossing the road. Which sign would you most likely see?

_____ 4. Your mother is driving you to your friend's house. You come to a busy street corner that has no traffic light. Which sign would help you get safely through the busy street corner?

_____ 5. In the car on your way to the beach you see a path crossing the road. People riding bikes and skating along the path need to cross the road. Which sign would you see?

_____ 6. Which sign would you probably see in all of these places: hospital; school; restaurant; courtroom; theater; library; playground; and museum.

©2008 Plutarch Publications, Inc. PPI-1003

Name _____   Standard: Forms/Signs

Many times in your life you will have to fill out forms. You need to fill out forms for things like getting a job, seeing a doctor, or buying a car.

Felix Sanchez is eight years old. His pet, a dog named Scruffy, is two years old. Scruffy is a male boxer. Felix and his father, Carlos Sanchez, took Scruffy to the vet, Dr. Bellos, for a check-up. Felix had to fill out a form before the vet could look at Scruffy.

1. Owner's name: _____
2. Owner's address: _____
3. Owner's phone number: _____
4. Type of pet: _____   5. Name of pet: _____
6. Age of pet: _____   7. Sex of pet: _____
8. Color of pet: _____
9. Has this pet visited the vet before? _____

1. From this form, will the vet know the pet's name? _____
2. Does the form give the vet's name? _____
3. What should Felix write on line 1?
   A. Scruffy   B. Felix Sanchez   C. Dr. Bellos
4. From this form, will the vet know how old the pet is? _____
5. From this form, will the vet know how many years Felix has owned Scruffy? _____
6. What should Felix write on line 6?
   A. two   B. seven   C. eight
7. From this card, will the vet know that the pet is a dog? _____
8. What WOULDN'T Felix write on line 8?
   A. brown   B. 555-1103   C. black and white
9. What should Felix write on line 7?
   A. male   B. female   C. dog

©2008 Plutarch Publications, Inc. PPI -1003

Name _____   Standard: Forms/Signs

> Many times in your life you will have to fill out forms.
> You need to fill out forms to get a job, go to the doctor,
> buy a car, and start at a new school.

Read the story below and use the information given to fill out the form.

Mr. Steve Townsend is a policeman. He got a new job in another city, bought a house, and moved his family there in June. His wife, Mindy, got a job as a teacher at Bedford Middle School. His children, Mark and Martha, are in the third grade at Parker School. Their new address is 107 Parkway Place, Dayton, Ohio, 49316. Their new phone number is 555-1742. Mark found a library only two blocks from his new home. The librarian asked him to fill out a form to get a new library card. Can you help Mark fill out the form?

1. Name _____
           Last   First

2. Address: _____
            Number   Street
            _____
            City   State   Zip Code

3. Phone number: _____

5. Name of your school: _____

6. Grade in school: _____

6. Name of parents or guardian: _____

7. Job of parents or guardian: _____

©2008 Plutarch Publications, Inc. PPI-1003

Name _____ Standard: Dictionary/Glossary

Words in a dictionary or glossary are listed in **alphabetical order** (ABC).

Can you put these two groups of words in alphabetical order?

limp	damp
hatch	guest
banana	admire
coast	inch
mistake	jolly
knife	enjoy
fancy	

unwrap	wobble
nature	tomato
zip	visitor
onion	power
reason	x-ray
safety	yawn
	quarter

1. _____
2. _____
3. _____
4. _____
5. _____
6. _____
7. _____
8. _____
9. _____
10. _____
11. _____
12. _____
13. _____

1. _____
2. _____
3. _____
4. _____
5. _____
6. _____
7. _____
8. _____
9. _____
10. _____
11. _____
12. _____
13. _____

©2008 Plutarch Publications, Inc. PPI -1003

Name _____   Standard: Dictionary/Glossary

A dictionary lists words in alphabetical order. It gives the **pronunciation** (how to say it), part of speech, and **definition**, or meaning.

Use this page from the dictionary to answer the questions below.

fail (fāl) *verb.* to not succeed or miss doing what was to be done
faint (fānt) *adjective.* to be weak, not strong, or unclear
fake (fāk) *verb.* to make something seem real in order to fool others
fame (fām) *noun.* being well known or much talked about
fellow (fel´o) *noun.* a man or boy
fierce (firs) *adjective.* wild or cruel
flare (fler) *verb.* to spread outward like a bell
fuss (fus) *noun.* too much bother or worry over a small thing

1. What is a *fake* jewel? A. a jewel that isn't real B. something valuable C. a diamond	2. Which word means "male"? A. fame B. fellow C. flare
3. Which word is a verb? A. faint B. fierce C. flare	4. What is a "definition"? A. how to say a word B. the meaning of a word C. the part of speech
5. Which word means "wild"? A. fake B. fame C. fierce	6. What part of speech is *fail*? A. verb B. adjective C. noun
7. What is a *fuss*? A. a long piece of string B. crying C. a big deal over nothing	8. Which person would have *fame*? A. a shy person B. a movie star C. a rabbit

©2008 Plutarch Publications, Inc. PPI-1003

Name _____   Standard: Dictionary/Glossary

A **GLOSSARY** is like a dictionary of special terms found at the back of a textbook like Science or Social Studies. The page number where the word is used in the book is given in parentheses ( ).

Read the glossary and use it to answer the questions below.

Glossary of Landforms:
canyon (22) - narrow valley with high steep sides
continent (18) - a very large mass of land covering the Earth
gulf (16) - part of the ocean that is almost surrounded by land
lake (13) - a large body of inland water
mountain (23) - large mass of land that rises above the surrounding land
ocean (12) - large body of water that covers most of the Earth
peak (23) - the pointed top of a mountain
peninsula (19) - a piece of land surrounded by water on three sides
plain (21) - large area of level or flat ground
stream (17) - a body of water that flows across the land

1. Are the words listed in alphabetical order? _____
2. What group of words are listed in this glossary?
   A. landforms   B. math words   C. oceans
3. What word means "the point at the top of a mountain"?
   A. canyon   B. peak   C. plain
4. On what page would the book talk about oceans?
   A. 11   B. 12   C. 18
5. Is a peninsula made of land or water? _____
6. Which two words can be found on page 23?
   A. ocean - stream   B. peak - canyon   C. mountain - peak
7. Which type of land is a large flat area?
   A. canyon   B. mountain   C. plain
8. Which type of water can be found inland?
   A. lake   B. gulf   C. ocean

©2008 Plutarch Publications, Inc. PPI -1003

ANSWER KEYS: 6, 7, 8, 9

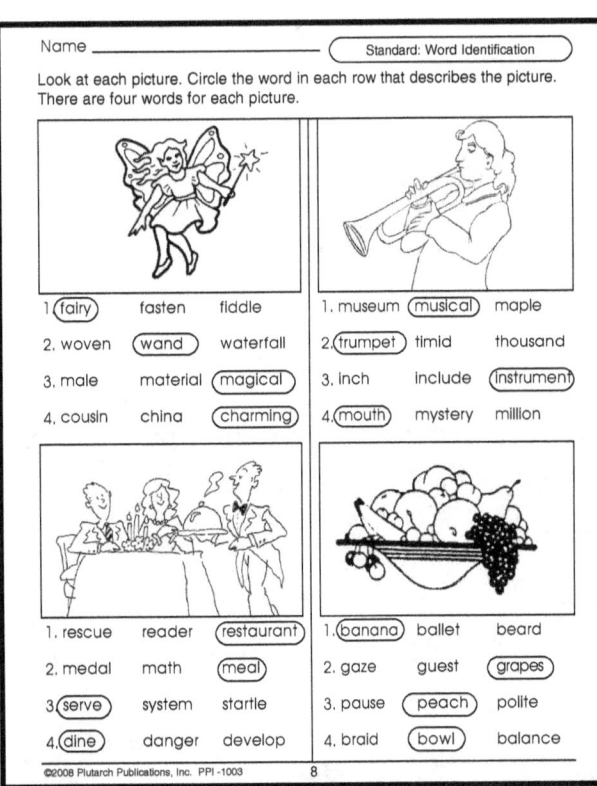

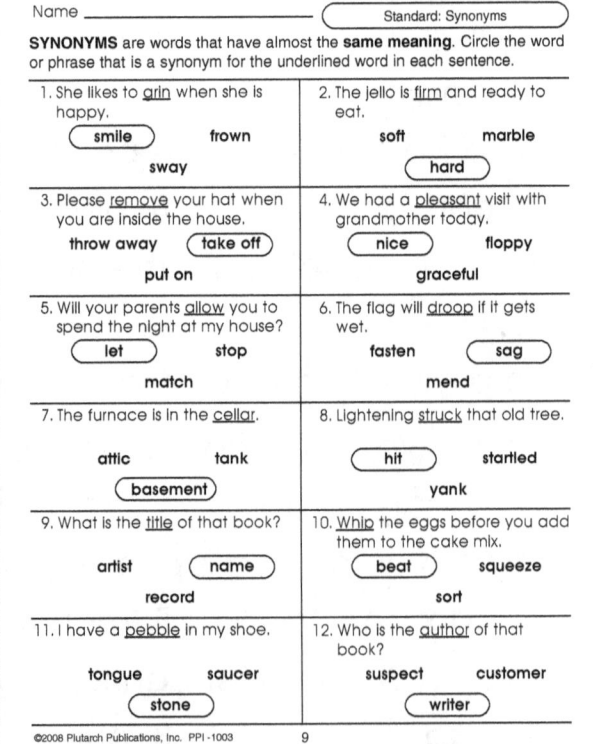

ANSWER KEYS: 10, 11, 12, 13

Worksheet 10 — Standard: Synonyms

SYNONYMS are words that have almost the **same meaning**. Circle the word or phrase that is a synonym for the underlined word in each sentence.

1. That sandwich tasted horrible!
   delicious — **(awful)** — favor

2. Kyle mowed his lawn last Saturday.
   (grass) — chimney — driveway

3. Wear a jacket because it is chilly today.
   example — **(coat)** — buggy

4. Brandon likes to boast about his soccer awards.
   (brag) — suggest — polish

5. I would like a couple of cookies please.
   three — **(two)** — none

6. Mother got a dozen roses from Father.
   split — **(twelve)** — thoughtful

7. Joey left his clothes in a heap on the floor.
   (pile) — drain — laundry

8. Please attach this page to your test.
   hush — **(fasten)** — nibble

9. Can you give me a hint about what my present will be?
   wrap — remind — **(clue)**

10. That wind feels icy today, so wear a scarf.
    (cold) — stubborn — worse

11. Can you mend the broken fence?
    (repair) — swirl — pinch

12. Who will paddle the canoe across the lake?
    remove — burst — **(row)**

Worksheet 11 — Standard: Synonyms

SYNONYMS are words that have almost the **same meaning**. Circle the word or phrase that is a synonym for the underlined word in each sentence.

1. I made a stupid mistake on this test.
   expert — **(dumb)** — design

2. Kelly's mother will guide us to the park.
   (lead) — demand — hatch

3. I am tired so it is time to quit working on this project.
   begin — **(stop)** — form

4. The car has a powerful engine that makes it go fast!
   brass — crisp — **(strong)**

5. Be gentle when you pet the puppy.
   rough — **(tender)** — marvelous

6. Did that wet vase harm the finish on the wooden table?
   (hurt) — label — obey

7. We need special equipment to cut down this tree.
   (tools) — fireworks — patterns

8. Sonja's family went to the coast for their vacation.
   gym — museum — **(seashore)**

9. The men found some ancient arrowheads in that field.
   object — dangerous — **(old)**

10. I weep when I peel onions!
    bleed — **(cry)** — study

11. We had a visitor in our classroom today.
    (guest) — servant — poet

12. My grandfather told me a tale of when he was a boy.
    telescope — fountain — **(story)**

Worksheet 12 — Standard: Antonyms

ANTONYMS are words that have **opposite meanings**. Circle the word or phrase that is an antonym for the underlined word in each sentence.

1. Three is an odd number.
   strange — double — **(even)**

2. It is time to say goodbye and leave now.
   ourselves — **(hello)** — foolish

3. Please pass your papers forward.
   around — **(backward)** — serious

4. The children were joyful when the party started.
   (sad) — slippery — complete

5. You can store that box beneath the bed.
   between — **(over)** — safety

6. We will continue to play the game until someone wins.
   (stop) — stumble — relax

7. Is that an actual medal from World War II?
   (fake) — true — brass

8. The dogs seemed to be calm during the rainstorm.
   comfortable — lazy — **(nervous)**

9. Sara's clothes got a little damp from the rain.
   (dry) — chilly — popular

10. China is a country faraway from here.
    distant — **(near)** — private

11. Ronda has a messy room that needs cleaning.
    tasty — peaceful — **(neat)**

12. Will the teacher excuse me for being so late to school?
    (punish) — suspect — sparkle

Worksheet 13 — Standard: Antonyms

ANTONYMS are words that have **opposite meanings**. Circle the word or phrase that is an antonym for the underlined word in each sentence.

1. That swift boat won the race!
   (slow) — stray — fisherman

2. Those two countries are at war because they don't agree.
   danger — battle — **(peace)**

3. That delicious food just seemed to vanish from the table!
   choke — **(appear)** — feast

4. You must twist the wire around this peg.
   scatter — sweep — **(straighten)**

5. It shows good manners when you are polite.
   (rude) — thrown — hopeful

6. This pool is too shallow for diving.
   narrow — **(deep)** — frozen

7. Jan plays with her imaginary friend.
   timid — backward — **(real)**

8. This is just an ordinary pencil.
   shaggy — **(unusual)** — plastic

9. Christie wore a fancy new dress to the party.
   marvelous — **(plain)** — gown

10. Judy lowered the shades to darken the room.
    (raised) — guarded — checked

11. May I borrow that book when you are finished?
    (lend) — chose — control

12. Sam was proud that he won the contest.
    eager — fearful — **(ashamed)**

ANSWER KEYS: 14, 15, 16, 17

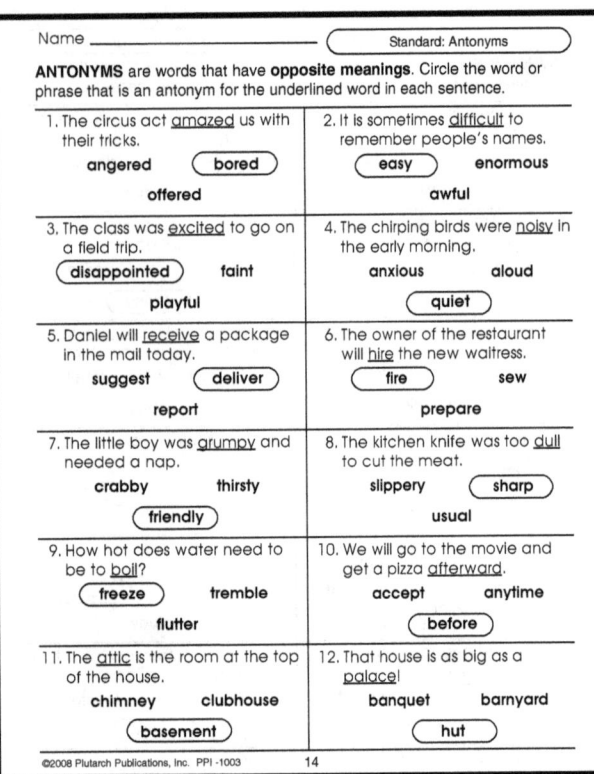

ANSWER KEYS: 18, 19, 20, 21

Worksheet 18

Name _____   Standard: Prefixes

A **PREFIX** is a group of letters placed in front of a word to change the meaning of that word. Each prefix has its own meaning. For example:

Prefix	Meaning	Example
"en"	to make	Enable "makes able".
"dis"	apart from, not	Distaste "does not taste good".
"un"	not	Unhappy means "not happy".
"mis"	wrong	Mistake means "take the wrong way".

Read each sentence then write the meaning of the underlined word on the blank below.

(ANSWERS MAY VARY)

1. Matt will enjoy his ice cream.
   MAKE JOYFUL OR FILL WITH JOY
2. Will this key unlock the door?
   NOT LOCK OR OPEN
3. The magician will make a rabbit disappear!
   NOT APPEAR OR GO AWAY
4. Do you think it is unfair to have to go to bed early?
   NOT FAIR
5. Please enclose a picture of yourself in your next letter to me.
   MAKE CLOSED OR SEAL INSIDE
6. Ryan disabled the radio when he took it apart.
   MADE NOT ABLE TO WORK
7. I misread the map and turned on the wrong street.
   READ WRONG
8. Sylvia is unlike her brother in many ways.
   NOT LIKE OR DIFFERENT
9. Did the dog misbehave when you left him home alone?
   BEHAVE WRONG OR ACT UP
10. Can you unfold those sheets for me?
    TAKE OUT THE FOLDS OR OPEN

Worksheet 19

Name _____   Standard: Prefixes

A **PREFIX** is a group of letters placed in front of a word to change the meaning of that word. Each prefix has its own meaning. For example:

Prefix	Meaning	Example
"non"	not	Nonsense "makes no sense".
"re"	back or again	Regain means "to gain back".
"pre"	before	Preheat means "to heat before using".
"sub"	under	Subway means "a way under".

Read each sentence then write the meaning of the underlined word on the blank below.

(ANSWERS MAY VARY)

1. Please refill the watering can for me.
   FILL AGAIN
2. We had a nonstop airplane flight to Denver.
   WITHOUT STOPPING
3. I grow these submarine plants in my fish tank.
   UNDER WATER
4. Shall we recount the votes to be sure who won?
   COUNT AGAIN
5. Drinking orange juice can help prevent a cold.
   STOP BEFORE IT HAPPENS
6. Use the nonstick pan to fry the hamburgers.
   WILL NOT STICK
7. I woke up predawn because I was excited about the party today.
   BEFORE THE SUN RISES
8. I like to read nonfiction books because they are about real people.
   NOT MADE UP
9. Will you please return the sweater that you borrowed last week?
   GIVE BACK
10. Do you recall where Sally lives?
    CALL BACK OR REMEMBER

Worksheet 20

Name _____   Standard: Prefixes

A **PREFIX** is a group of letters placed in front of a word to change the meaning of that word. Each prefix has its own meaning. For example:

Prefix	Meaning	Example
"com"	with, together	Combine means "put together".
"im"	not, never	Impassable means "not able to pass".
"bi"	two	Bisect means "to cut in two pieces".
"over"	too much or across	Overused means "used too much".

Read each sentence then write the meaning of the underlined word on the blank below.

(ANSWERS MAY VARY)

1. Did the catcher overthrow the ball to second base?
   THROW TOO FAR
2. Mother compresses her lips when she gets angry.
   PRESSES TOGETHER
3. It is impossible to draw a perfect picture of yourself!
   NOT POSSIBLE
4. My bicycle has a flat tire.
   HAVING TWO WHEELS
5. After only one year the garden was overgrown.
   GREW TO MUCH
6. There was so much rain the river began to overflow its banks.
   FLOW OVER THE SIDE
7. The storm passed overnight and the sun was shining this morning.
   THROUGH THE NIGHT
8. It is impolite to speak when your mouth is full of food.
   NOT POLITE
9. I will compose a photo of different types of flowers.
   POSE OR PUT TOGETHER
10. Brandon flew overseas to see his aunt and uncle.
    ACROSS THE SEA OR OCEAN

Worksheet 21

Name _____   Standard: Suffixes

A **SUFFIX** is a group of letters placed behind a word to change the meaning of that word. Each suffix has its own meaning. For example:

Suffix	Meaning	Example
"ness"	state of being	Sickness means "being sick or ill".
"en"	made of	Brighten means "made bright".
"ern"	of a direction	Western means "part of the west".
"s"	more than one	Closets means "more than one closet".

Read each sentence then write the meaning of the underlined word on the blank below.

(ANSWERS MAY VARY)

1. When Kate's dog was lost, she was filled with sadness.
   VERY SAD
2. Mike found fossils of bird bones when he dug the hole in the yard.
   MORE THAN ONE FOSSIL
3. Please darken the room so that we can watch the movie.
   MAKE DARKER
4. How many pumpkins do I need to make a pie?
   MORE THAN ONE PUMPKIN
5. Carrie is sweet and has goodness in her heart.
   BEING GOOD
6. My classroom has seven computers for the students to use.
   MORE THAN ONE COMPUTER
7. Louisiana is a southern state.
   PART OF THE SOUTH
8. The glue must harden before we can use the broken cup again.
   LET IT BECOME HARD
9. The sun rises in the eastern sky every morning.
   PART OF THE EAST
10. There are some loose threads hanging from your sleeve.
    MORE THAN ONE THREAD

©2008 Plutarch Publications, Inc. PPI-1003

ANSWER KEYS: 22, 23, 24, 25

Name _____   Standard: Suffixes

A **SUFFIX** is a group of letters placed behind a word to change the meaning of that word. Each suffix has its own meaning. For example:

"ful" - full of	Cheer**ful** means "full of cheer".
"less" - without	Care**less** means "without care".
"ly" - in what manner	Excited**ly** means "in an excited way".
"ous" - full of	Vari**ous** means "full of variety".

Read each sentence then write the meaning of the underlined word on the blank below. **(ANSWERS MAY VARY)**

1. The dog was <u>fearless</u> as he faced the raccoon.
   WITHOUT FEAR
2. It is <u>helpful</u> to have more than one pencil during a test.
   FULL OF HELP
3. Mrs. Green <u>nicely</u> offered us a piece of pie!
   IN A NICE WAY
4. That artwork is <u>colorful</u> and interesting!
   FULL OF COLOR
5. Dean <u>politely</u> asked if he could have another cookie.
   IN A POLITE WAY
6. The <u>dangerous</u> road had many curves and steep hills.
   FULL OF DANGER
7. Greg was <u>hopeful</u> that he made the football team.
   FULL OF HOPE
8. Watching those dark clouds over the lake makes me <u>nervous</u>.
   FULL OF NERVES
9. The old newspapers were <u>worthless</u> so no one wanted them.
   WITHOUT VALUE OR WORTH
10. <u>Slowly</u> open your eyes so the bright sun doesn't hurt them.
    IN A SLOW MANNER

©2008 Plutarch Publications, Inc. PPI -1003   22

Name _____   Standard: Suffixes

A **SUFFIX** is a group of letters placed behind a word to change the meaning of that word. Each suffix has its own meaning. For example:

"ship" - state or quality	Hard**ship** means "in a state of hard times".
"able" - worth or ability	Love**able** means "worth loving".
"like" - relating to	Home**like** means "relating to home or like home".
"er" - a person who	Explor**er** means "a person who explores".

Read each sentence then write the meaning of the underlined word on the blank below. **(ANSWERS MAY VARY)**

1. Our <u>friendship</u> will last for many years.
   THE STATE OF BEING FRIENDS
2. Mr. Wilder becomes <u>childlike</u> when he goes to a circus!
   LIKE A CHILD
3. Jose is the <u>pitcher</u> for our baseball team.
   PERSON WHO PITCHES
4. This bed is so <u>comfortable</u> I overslept this morning!
   FULL OF COMFORT
5. We took <u>ownership</u> when we bought that car.
   THE STATE OF OWNING
6. Gustav is a <u>dependable</u> worker.
   ABLE TO BE DEPENDED ON
7. That child <u>performer</u> can sing and dance very well.
   PERSON WHO PERFORMS
8. The problem is <u>solvable</u> if we put our heads together and think.
   ABLE TO BE SOLVED
9. The <u>traveler</u> drove through five states to visit his friend.
   PERSON TRAVELING
10. Can you believe how <u>lifelike</u> those silk flowers look?
    ALMOST LOOK ALIVE

©2008 Plutarch Publications, Inc. PPI -1003   23

Name _____   Standard: Figurative Language

FIGURATIVE LANGUAGE is a colorful way to express an idea by drawing a picture with words and giving us a new way to see something. For example:
"It is raining cats and dogs!"
This does not mean that cats and dogs are falling from the sky. It makes an image exaggerating the amount of rain that is falling.

Each sentence below uses figurative language. Circle the choice that tells what the sentence really means.

1. Gretchen stood as still as a statue.
   Gretchen was frozen in ice.   Gretchen was asleep.
   (Gretchen was standing very still.)
2. Mr. Smith roared when the baseball broke his window.
   Mr. Smith was a lion.   **(Mr. Smith yelled.)**
   Mr. Smith was very sad.
3. Rosemary has cheeks like roses!
   (Rosemary's cheeks are red.)   Rosemary smells good.
   Rosemary has big cheeks.
4. My head is pounding like a bass drum.
   I am sick to my stomach.   **(I have a bad headache.)**
   I like to listen to music.
5. That basketball player is a skyscraper!
   The basketball player is quiet.   **(The basketball player is tall.)**
   The basketball player lives in the city.
6. Dan's house is like an oven today.
   (Dan's house is hot.)   Dan is baking cookies.
   Dan lives in the desert.

©2008 Plutarch Publications, Inc. PPI -1003   24

Name _____   Standard: Figurative Language

FIGURATIVE LANGUAGE is a colorful way to express an idea by drawing a picture with words and giving us a new way to see something. For example:
"Patty is as quiet as a mouse."
This does not mean that Patty cannot talk or make noise. It makes an image exaggerating how quiet Patty is.

Each sentence below uses figurative language. Circle the choice that tells what the sentence really means

1. Mitchell piled his ice cream a mile high!
   (Mitchell took a lot of ice cream.)   The ice cream was cold.
   Mitchell was in an airplane.
2. Kristie strained her brain studying for the big test.
   Kristie had a headache.   **(Kristie studied hard.)**
   Kristie could not study.
3. This day has been a million years long!
   The day went by quickly.   The day was over.
   (It was a long day.)
4. Sandy's hands are like ice cubes.
   (Sandy has cold hands.)   Sandy is standing in snow.
   Sandy's hands are in her pockets.
5. The baby slept like a rock after playtime.
   The baby was snoring.   The baby cried.
   (The baby was tired and slept well.)
6. Nancy's hair is like velvet.
   Nancy's hair is tangled.   **(Nancy's hair is soft.)**
   Nancy has short curly hair.

©2008 Plutarch Publications, Inc. PPI -1003   25

©2008 Plutarch Publications, Inc. PPI -1003

ANSWER KEYS: 26, 27, 28, 29

Name _____ Standard: Context Clues

Put an **X** in the box beside the word that best completes each sentence.

1. Boil water in the _____ for tea.
   - ☐ kiss   ☒ kettle   ☐ key
2. The workman wears a _____ to protect his head.
   - ☒ helmet   ☐ hospital   ☐ hunter
3. The _____ wanted to buy a loaf of bread.
   - ☐ churn   ☐ capture   ☒ customer
4. The _____ child was afraid of everything.
   - ☐ treasure   ☐ tennis   ☒ timid
5. Is it time to _____ your birthday?
   - ☐ clatter   ☒ celebrate   ☐ command
6. The warm sun and cool breeze make this a _____ day.
   - ☒ pleasant   ☐ pebble   ☐ package
7. You must come in through the _____, not the exit.
   - ☐ expert   ☐ emergency   ☒ entrance
8. King Roy had a green _____ in his crown.
   - ☒ jewel   ☐ jelly   ☐ jaw
9. Does Randy know how to _____ that machine?
   - ☐ object   ☒ operate   ☐ occur
10. Marcy _____ chewing gum.
    - ☐ quiet   ☐ quarter   ☒ quit

26

Name _____ Standard: Context Clues

Put an **X** in the box beside the word that best completes each sentence.

1. We will go on an _____ in the jungle!
   - ☐ address   ☒ adventure   ☐ admire
2. The lion had a _____ growl!
   - ☐ flame   ☒ fierce   ☐ fever
3. There is a flower box on the window _____.
   - ☐ listener   ☐ lawn   ☒ ledge
4. The _____ train arrived two hours early!
   - ☒ rapid   ☐ remain   ☐ route
5. Wendy felt _____ as she waited for the principal.
   - ☒ anxious   ☐ accept   ☐ approach
6. Do not worry about the _____ until it gets here!
   - ☐ forty   ☐ further   ☒ future
7. Smog and smoke are kinds of _____.
   - ☐ polish   ☒ pollution   ☐ precious
8. The pinwheel began to _____ in colorful circles.
   - ☐ waste   ☒ whirl   ☐ wrinkle
9. Mack was _____ to go play at the beach.
   - ☐ entire   ☒ eager   ☐ excuse
10. Study hard and you will _____ your grades!
    - ☒ improve   ☐ immediate   ☐ insist

27

Name _____ Standard: Context Clues

Put an **X** in the box beside the word that best completes each sentence.

1. Be sure to _____ those dirty dishes!
   - ☐ sharpen   ☐ slippery   ☒ scrub
2. My pencil is very _____, just like yours.
   - ☐ otherwise   ☒ ordinary   ☐ offer
3. Watch the speed _____ and go slowly here.
   - ☐ laundry   ☒ limit   ☐ liquid
4. Don't _____ about having to clean your room!
   - ☐ grind   ☐ gentle   ☒ grumble
5. That _____ puppy tore the newspaper.
   - ☒ naughty   ☐ needle   ☐ national
6. We went to the _____ to see that new movie.
   - ☒ theater   ☐ traffic   ☐ tunnel
7. The explorers went on a _____ to the North Pole.
   - ☐ jerk   ☒ journey   ☐ judge
8. Would you like to _____ on some popcorn?
   - ☐ material   ☐ motion   ☒ munch
9. Did you _____ your present yet?
   - ☒ unwrap   ☐ usual   ☐ underneath
10. _____ the secret message after you read it!
    - ☐ Skunk   ☒ Shred   ☐ Safety

28

Name _____ Standard: Context Clues

Put an **X** in the box beside the word that best completes each sentence.

1. The firemen will _____ the cat in the tree.
   - ☐ recipe   ☐ rocket   ☒ rescue
2. I can always _____ on my best friend!
   - ☐ danger   ☒ depend   ☐ drawn
3. Alice likes to _____ at the flowers in the garden.
   - ☒ gaze   ☐ graceful   ☐ glitter
4. Put a _____ of sticks on the campfire.
   - ☐ biscuit   ☐ bounce   ☒ bundle
5. Preston will _____ the treehouse by himself!
   - ☐ delicate   ☒ design   ☐ droop
6. Did I _____ that I am very hungry?
   - ☒ mention   ☐ magical   ☐ memory
7. In the fall, we _____ the ripe crops.
   - ☐ harbor   ☒ harvest   ☐ hatch
8. Piper will go to the _____ with her parents.
   - ☒ banquet   ☐ beard   ☐ burst
9. Can you _____ an enormous hill of jelly beans?
   - ☐ intelligent   ☐ impatient   ☒ imagine
10. The rabbit began to _____ on the tender lettuce.
    - ☐ nonsense   ☐ narrow   ☒ nibble

29

©2008 PLUTARCH PUBLICATIONS, INC. PPI-1003   75

ANSWER KEYS: 30, 31, 32, 33

Name _____ *Standard: Sequence of Events*

Sequence of Events is the order in which things happen. Signal words like first, second, then, next, after, and finally help show the order of events. Read the stories then number the events in the correct sequence.

I am excited! This year at school I have a locker with a combination lock. First I have to spin the dial three times to the left. Next I turn right and point the arrow to the number 33. After that, I turn the dial left one full turn and stop on the number 41. I then turn the dial right and stop at the number 57. The next thing I do is pull on the lock and it opens. Finally, I pull up on the handle and open my locker. I can keep my coat and books in the locker instead of in my desk!

Open the lock:
- **2** Turn right to number 33.
- **5** Turn right to number 57.
- **7** Pull up on the handle.
- **8** Open my locker.
- **1** Spin three times to the left.
- **4** Stop on the number 41.
- **3** Turn left one full turn.
- **6** Pull to open the lock.

Make a pizza:
- **1** Get out all the ingredients.
- **3** Spread on the sauce.
- **5** Add cheese.
- **8** Eat the pizza.
- **4** Add pepperoni.
- **7** Let cool for one minute.
- **6** Cook for two minutes.
- **2** Put the muffin on a plate.

Darren's favorite snack is pizza that he makes himself. The first thing he does is set all the ingredients on the kitchen counter. Next he puts an English muffin on a paper plate. He spreads the muffin with tomato sauce. After that he puts on pepperoni and then cheese. Darren puts the pizza in the microwave for two minutes. He takes the pizza out of the microwave and lets it cool for one minute. He pours a glass of milk. At last he can take a big bite of the home-made pizza!

©2008 Plutarch Publications, Inc. PPI -1003   30

Name _____ *Standard: Sequence of Events*

Sequence of Events is the order in which things happen. Signal words like first, second, then, next, after, and finally help show the order of events. Read the stories then number the events in the correct sequence.

To get the best grades and learn well, you should prepare a place to study. First, find a table that you can use. Clear off a spot for your books and paper. Make sure there is a lamp or light so you can see to read. Put your books on the table. Set out your paper and pencil to take notes. Pull up a comfortable chair. Begin to read and take notes. Be sure to take a break about every twenty minutes so you don't get too tired. Study for an hour or two. Good luck on your tests!

Ready for homework:
- **4** Set your books on the table.
- **7** Read and take notes.
- **5** Put out paper and pencils.
- **8** Take a break.
- **3** Turn on a lamp or light.
- **2** Clear off a spot on the table.
- **1** Find a table.
- **6** Get a comfortable chair.

Set the table:
- **4** Forks go on each napkin.
- **3** Put the napkins on the left.
- **7** Glasses go above the forks.
- **6** Spoons go next to the knives.
- **1** Set the plates on the table.
- **2** Fold the napkins.
- **5** Knives are set to the right.
- **8** Set flowers on the table.

Josie helps her mother by setting the table for dinner every night. First, Josie sets out the plates. She folds napkins then sets them to the left of each plate. Josie puts a fork on each napkin. Then she puts a bread knife on the right side of every plate. After that she puts a spoon next to each knife. When those things are done, Josie places a glass above the forks at each place setting. The last thing Josie does is set a vase of flowers in the middle of the table.

©2008 Plutarch Publications, Inc. PPI -1003   31

Name _____ *Standard: Referents*

REFERENTS are words that take the place of a word so you don't have to repeat it many times. *She, it, they, he, a few, some,* and *we* are some of the referents we use. For example:
   Betty is running for class president. <u>She</u> wants to win the race!
The word "She" refers to Betty without having to name her again.

Read the sentences below. Circle the word in the second sentence that stands for the underlined word or words in the first sentence.

1. <u>The people in my family</u> have many talents. (They) are artists!
2. <u>My mother</u> paints. (She) likes to paint portraits of people.
3. Mother paints with <u>watercolors</u>. (They) are easy to use and look nice.
4. <u>Grandpa</u> works with wood. (He) carves things out of sticks.
5. He has entered <u>his carvings</u> in contests. (They) often win prizes.
6. Designing gardens is what my <u>father</u> does. (He) likes working outdoors.
7. Father puts many <u>roses</u> in his gardens. He thinks (they) are beautiful.
8. <u>Grandma</u> is a florist. (She) arranges flowers and delivers them to customers.
9. Sometimes Grandma uses flowers from <u>Father's</u> gardens. She thinks (his) flowers are very colorful and nice.
10. My sister, <u>Katie</u>, is a dancer. (Her) class performs once a month.
11. They dance at the <u>theater</u> in town. (It) has an enormous stage.
12. <u>My whole family</u> goes to watch. (We) clap for Katie when the show is over.
13. <u>My talent</u> is very unusual. (It) takes a lot of patience and love.
14. My talent is cooking delicious <u>meals</u>. Everyone likes eating (them)!

©2008 Plutarch Publications, Inc. PPI -1003   32

Name _____ *Standard: Referents*

REFERENTS are words that take the place of a word so you don't have to repeat it many times. *She, it, they, he, a few, some,* and *we* are some of the referents we use. For example:
   The cat is sleeping in the basket. He likes to sleep <u>there</u>.
The word "there" refers to "in the basket", the place where the cat sleeps.

Read each pair of sentences. On the line, write the word or words that refer to the underlined word.

1. Jack and Jake had an adventure today. <u>They</u> went on a hike to the lake in the park.
   They _____ **JACK AND JAKE**
2. The boys packed a picnic lunch. <u>They</u> rode bicycles all the way to the lake.
   They _____ **THE BOYS**
3. When they got to the lake, Jack wanted to take a swim. The water was a little cold, but <u>he</u> wanted to jump in right away.
   He _____ **JACK**
4. Jake saw a boat in some bushes near the water. He thought <u>it</u> looked a little old, but strong enough to stay afloat.
   it _____ **A BOAT**
5. Jack wasn't sure that the boat was safe. <u>He</u> said the boards looked a little weak.
   He _____ **JACK**
6. Jack and Jake put the boat into the shallow water and got in. <u>The two of them</u> waited for a few minutes.
   The two of them _____ **JACK AND JAKE**
7. The boat began to fill up with water. Before long, <u>it</u> was up to the boy's ankles.
   it _____ **WATER**
8. Jake jumped out and dragged the boat back to shore. The boys agreed <u>it</u> was not safe enough to take for a ride across the lake!
   it _____ **THE BOAT**

©2008 Plutarch Publications, Inc. PPI -1003   33

ANSWER KEYS: 34, 35, 36, 37

Name _____   Standard: Compare/Contrast

We **compare** and **contrast** things to find out
how they are **alike** and how they are **different**.

cup   glass

Read each statement below. If the statement describes the cup, write
C on the line. If the statement describes the glass, write **G** on the line. If
the statement describes both items, write **B** on the line.

__C__ 1. I have a handle.
__G__ 2. I am taller.
__B__ 3. You can put liquid in me.
__B__ 4. You can drink from me.
__B__ 5. I am found in the kitchen.
__G__ 6. You often put cold water or milk in me.
__C__ 7. I am usually used for hot liquid.
__C__ 8. I have a saucer.
__B__ 9. I have a lip or rim around my top.
__C__ 10. I look like half of a ball.
__G__ 11. I am taller than I am wide.
__C__ 12. I am shorter.
__B__ 13. From the top view I look round.
__C__ 14. Adults use me for coffee or tea.
__B__ 15. I can be cleaned in the dishwasher.

©2008 Plutarch Publications, Inc. PPI-1003   34

Name _____   Standard: Compare/Contrast

We **compare** and **contrast** things to find out
how they are **alike** and how they are **different**.

nickel   dime

Read each statement below. If the statement describes the nickel,
write **N** on the line. If the statement describes the dime, write **D** on the
line. If the statement describes both items, write **B** on the line.

__B__ 1. I am a coin.
__B__ 2. You can buy things with me.
__D__ 3. I am worth more money than the other coin.
__B__ 4. I have a "head" and a "tail".
__N__ 5. My President is facing right.
__N__ 6. I have a larger size than the other coin.
__N__ 7. I am worth five pennies.
__D__ 8. My President is facing left.
__D__ 9. I am worth ten pennies.
__B__ 10. I am round.
__B__ 11. I am flat.
__D__ 12. I have a smaller size than the other coin.
__B__ 13. I have a date stamped on me.
__B__ 14. People use me.
__B__ 15. I am made of metal.

©2008 Plutarch Publications, Inc. PPI-1003   35

Name _____   Standard: Compare/Contrast

We **compare** and **contrast** things to find out
how they are **alike** and how they are **different**.

corn   watermelon

Read each statement below. If the statement describes the corn, write
C on the line. If the statement describes the watermelon, write **S** on the
line. If the statement describes both items, write **B** on the line.

__W__ 1. I am round and red inside.
__B__ 2. People eat me.
__C__ 3. I have a papery husk covering my yellow inside.
__B__ 4. I have a green covering.
__W__ 5. I am wet and juicy.
__W__ 6. Many people like to spit my seeds.
__C__ 7. I have yellow kernels.
__C__ 8. I am a vegetable.
__W__ 9. I can be squeezed and made into a tasty breakfast drink.
__C__ 10. I grow on tall stalks.
__B__ 11. I am delicious.
__C__ 12. You should cook me before I am eaten.
__W__ 13. I am in the fruit family.
__B__ 14. I come from a plant.
__C__ 15. I am served hot.

©2008 Plutarch Publications, Inc. PPI-1003   36

Name _____   Standard: Cause and Effect

CAUSE is something that happens and **EFFECT** is the result. For example:

Brian was hungry, so Mara made him a turkey sandwich.

The event that happened, or CAUSE, was that Brian was hungry.
The result, or EFFECT, was that Mara made a sandwich.

In each sentence below, underline the cause and circle the effect.

1. Casey didn't have a book to read, (so he went to the library.)
2. (He had to wait outside for ten minutes) because the library wasn't open yet.
3. (The librarian opened the door) because she arrived with the key.
4. She had several books in her arms (so Casey held the door for her.)
5. (The librarian smiled and thanked him) because he was so polite.
6. Casey didn't know where begin looking (so he asked for some help.)
7. Because he didn't know what kind of book to read, (the librarian asked if he liked fiction or nonfiction better.)
8. Casey usually read nonfiction, (so he told the librarian he liked history books about inventions.)
9. (The librarian smiled) because she knew just where to look.
10. The librarian led him to the shelves with books about inventions, (and Casey was excited to have so many choices!)
11. Because Casey looked at all the books, (he found just the one he wanted.)
12. Casey had found just the right book (which pleased the librarian.)

©2008 Plutarch Publications, Inc. PPI-1003   37

ANSWER KEYS: 38, 39, 40, 41

Name _____ Standard: Cause and Effect

CAUSE is something that happens and **EFFECT** is the result. For example:
(The carpet was wet) because Liam spilled his glass of juice.
The event that happened, or CAUSE, was that Liam spilled juice.
The result, or EFFECT, was that the carpet was wet.

In each sentence below, underline the cause and circle the effect.

1. (Flashy, a little fish, was sad) because he had no one to play with.
2. Because the water was sunny and bright, (it looked like a great day to play and have a grand adventure!)
3. Flashy couldn't see any friends outside, (so he went to find them.)
4. Finny's house was dark, (so Flashy knew no one was home.)
5. (Bubble's Mother came to the door) when Flashy knocked.
6. She said Bubbles wasn't feeling well (so she couldn't come out to play.)
7. Because he was gone to his swimming lessons, (Flashy's friend Octy couldn't play either.)
8. (Flashy was sad) because his friends could not play with him.
9. (He swam in slow circles) because he did not know what else to do.
10. Flashy looked down at the sand beneath him, (and that made him notice his shadow below.)
11. Since there was no one else around, (Flashy decided to play tag with his own shadow!)
12. (Flashy was finally happy) because the sun had given him a friend!

Name _____ Standard: Conclude/Predict

Sometimes the events in a story can give clues as to what is going to happen. You can use those clues to **PREDICT**, or tell what might happen next.
Read each paragraph below and predict what will probably happen next. Circle your answer.

1. Levi and Josh were playing ball. Levi said he could throw the ball farther than Josh. Josh said that he could throw the ball farther. What will probably happen?
   A. The boys will go home and watch television.
   B. The boys will take turns trying to throw the ball as far as they can.
   C. The boys will play a game of baseball.

2. Marge was drinking grape juice in the living room where she wasn't supposed to eat or drink. Marge spilled her glass of juice on the carpet. It left a big purple stain. What will probably happen?
   A. Marge's parents will bring her a present.
   B. The stain will disappear by itself.
   C. Marge's parents will be upset with her.

3. Dark clouds were gathering overhead. It began to thunder and the wind started to blow. Lightning flashed across the sky! What will probably happen?
   A. It will rain.
   B. It will snow.
   C. A rainbow will appear.

4. Craig could hear his mother in the kitchen. He sniffed deeply as good smells drifted from the kitchen. Craig set plates, glasses, and napkins on the table. What will probably happen?
   A. The family will watch a movie.
   B. The family will sit down to eat.
   C. Craig will fall asleep on the couch.

Name _____ Standard: Conclude/Predict

Often, you can use your own experiences to understand even more than the author tells you. That is called **DRAWING CONCLUSIONS**.

Read each paragraph below and answer the question by DRAWING A CONCLUSION. Circle your answer.

1. Amy stood in her backyard with the leash in her hand. She looked everywhere, but she could not find her dog. She called "Sparky! Come here, Sparky!" but there was no answer. How is Amy feeling?
   A. Amy is happy that she can't find her dog.
   B. Amy is worried that the dog is lost.
   C. Amy is sleepy.

2. Marcus yawned and stretched, then pushed back the blanket. The smell of pancakes and bacon drifted in from the kitchen. Marcus jumped out of bed. What time of day is it?
   A. It is morning.
   B. It is late at night and time to go to bed.
   C. It is after school.

3. Randy rubbed his cold hands together and wished he had brought his gloves. His boots and jacket were warm, but his hood was not snug enough to cover his ears. What is the weather like?
   A. It is raining.
   B. It is warm and breezy.
   C. It is cold and maybe snowing.

4. Emily and Chris each got a tray and stood in line. As they moved forward, Emily took a salad but Chris chose a bowl of peaches. They both took the ham and mashed potatoes. Where are they?
   A. Emily and Chris are at the movie theater.
   B. Emily and Chris are in the lunch line at school.
   C. Emily and Chris are having a picnic in the park.

Name _____ Standard: Author's Purpose

Authors have a **PURPOSE**, or reason, for the things they write. One purpose is to tell facts or true stories. Another purpose is to amuse or entertain the reader.

Tell the PURPOSE for each type of written work listed. Write **F** on the line if the purpose is to give facts or information. Write **A** if the purpose is to entertain.

- **F** 1. newspaper story about the mayor
- **A** 2. book of jokes
- **F** 3. Science book
- **A** 4. comic strip in the newspaper
- **A** 5. book of poems
- **A** 6. nursery rhymes
- **F** 7. dictionary
- **A** 8. comic book
- **A** 9. story about a rabbit that talks
- **F** 10. story about Abraham Lincoln
- **A** 11. mystery story
- **F** 12. book about planets and stars
- **F** 13. Math book
- **A** 14. fashion magazine
- **F** 15. book about your state
- **A** 16. fairy tales
- **F** 17. book about whales and sharks
- **F** 18. an article about the President
- **F** 19. cook book
- **F** 20. guide for learning about computers

ANSWER KEYS: 42, 43, 44, 45

Standard: Genre

Genre is the style in which a story is written. Three types of genre are:
Fantasy - characters can do things they never could in the real world
Biography - the life story about a real person
Fairy Tale - imaginary creatures and magic with a happy ending

Read the statements below. On the line write **F** if the book is fantasy, **B** if it is a biography, and **FT** if it is a fairy tale.

__F__ 1. *Amanda Pig and Her Big Brother Oliver,* by Jean Van Leeuwen, is a story about a pig named Oliver and his troubles with his little sister, Amanda, who always follows him around.

__B__ 2. *Wanted Dead or Alive: the True Story of Harriet Tubman,* by Ann McGovern, tells the story of a female slave who escapes to freedom. Then she helps other slaves become free.

__FT__ 3. *Rapunzel,* by Bernice Chardiet, is the story of a princess with long hair who is put under a magic spell by a wicked witch. The girl is locked in a tower and rescued by a prince.

__F__ 4. *Day of the Dragon King,* by Mary Pope Osborne, is an exciting story about two children who have a treehouse that takes them back in time. They go back to ancient China on a mission to find a book and save the library.

__B__ 5. *Louisa May Alcott: Young Novelist,* by Beatrice Gormley, is the story of Louisa's childhood. Her family was poor and she almost died, but she grew up to become a famous author.

__FT__ 6. *Rumpelstiltskin,* by the brothers Grimm, is the story of an odd looking little man who saves a princess by spinning hay into gold. The princess has to give the man her first child unless she can guess his name.

Standard: Narrative Comprehension

My name is Matt. I live in a small town in **Iowa**, a state in the north. There are thirty-two people in the **entire**, or whole, third grade at school! There are many good things about having such a small class. I know everyone and they all know me. I can walk all the way across town in less than fifteen minutes, so getting around is easy. Living in a small town is like having one big family. We all watch out for each other and help each other. There are some problems with living in a small town. We only have one grocery store, bank, restaurant and gas station. There is no place to buy clothes so we must drive to a city nearby for that kind of shopping or to go to a movie. But, living in a small town makes me feel safe and comfortable. I wouldn't want to live anywhere else!

1. What is the name of the boy in the story? __MATT__
2. In which state does he live? __IOWA__

Name three things the boy likes about living in a small town.
3. __HE KNOWS EVERYBODY__
4. __IT IS EASY TO GET AROUND TOWN__   (ANSWERS MAY VARY)
5. __IT IS LIKE HAVING A BIG FAMILY__

6. What is not so good about living in a small town?
__THERE ARE NOT MANY STORES OR PLACES TO GO IN A SMALL TOWN__

7. What does the word "entire" mean?
   A. tired   (B. whole)   C. small
8. What would be a good title for this story?
   A. A Boy Named Matt
   (B. Living in a Small Town)
   C. City Life

Find it: Find Iowa on a map of the United States.
Imagine it: What is it like living in a small town?

Standard: Narrative Comprehension

Isabela lives with her grandmother and grandfather in the western state of **Arizona**. They live in a town near the **desert**, a warm dry area with lots of sand. Isabela and her grandmother enjoy having picnics in the desert. They like to pack a lunch and ride their horses into the desert. They look at the different **cacti**, or plants that grow well in the desert because they don't need much water. The tall **saguaro** cactus looks like it has many branches reaching up into the wide blue sky! Isabela and grandmother often sit in the shade of that large plant when they stop for lunch. Isabela loves living near the desert, even though the weather is hot and dry. At night it cools down and every star shines brightly in the dark desert sky.

1. What is the name of the girl in the story? __ISABELA__
2. In which state does she live? __ARIZONA__

Name three things the story tells you about the desert.
3. __IT IS A WARM, DRY AREA OF LAND__
4. __CACTI GROW IN THE DESERT__   (ANSWERS MAY VARY)
5. __THE DESERT COOLS OFF AT NIGHT__

6. What is a "saguaro"?
__A TYPE OF CACTUS THAT LIVES IN THE DESERT. IT IS A LARGE PLANT WITH MANY BRANCHES.__

7. What is a "desert"?
   A. a sweet treat   B. saguaro   (C. a warm dry land)
8. What would be a good title for this story?
   A. Isabela and the Horses
   B. Grandmother Makes a Picnic
   (C. Fun In The Desert)

Find it: Find Arizona on a map of the United States.
Compare it: How are the desert and your town alike?

Standard: Narrative Comprehension

Ben and his friends are going swimming today. They live in **Florida** near the ocean and like to spend their summer days at the beach. Ben will bring his swim mask and **snorkel**, a tube that lets him breathe underwater. Randy and Joe will bring their snorkels, too. The boys will swim in the **shallow** water, where it is not deep, and look at all the plants and animals. Sometimes they will see schools of brightly colored fish. Other times they find small animals among the long seaweed that grows there. When they are tired of swimming, they like to explore along the beach. They find shells and smooth bits of wood that have washed up on the shore. The three boys end the day by building a giant sandcastle!

1. Who is the main character in this story? __BEN__
2. In which state does he live? __FLORIDA__

Name three things the boys can do at the beach.
3. __SWIM__
4. __LOOK FOR SHELLS__   (ANSWERS MAY VARY)
5. __BUILD A SANDCASTLE__

6. What is a "snorkel"?
__A TUBE USED FOR BREATHING UNDERWATER__

7. What does the word "shallow" mean?
   (A. not deep)   B. deep   C. colorful fish
8. What would be a good title for this story?
   (A. A Day at the Beach)
   B. Ben Goes Swimming
   C. How to Build a Sandcastle

Find it: Find Florida on a map of the United States.
Think about it: What do you like to do at the beach?

ANSWER KEYS: 46, 47, 48, 49

Worksheet 46

Name _____ Standard: Narrative Comprehension

Winona lives in the Black Hills of **South Dakota**. The hills are covered with tall dark pine trees, and from far away that makes the hills look black! Winona's best friend is Wapi, her **cousin** (the child her aunt and uncle). Winona and Wapi often like to hike in the woods near their home. They walk quietly so they don't scare away the animals that live there. Winona takes a camera and gets a picture of the animals they find. Wapi brings a notebook and pencil so he can takes notes to remember where they saw each animal. When they get home, Winona and Wapi take out their photo album and add the new pictures and notes. They have pictures of deer, mountain goats, a gopher, and even a **bison** (an animal that looks like a buffalo).

1. Who is the main character in this story? __WINONA__
2. In which state does she live? __SOUTH DAKOTA__

Name three animals pictured in the photo album.
3. __DEER__
4. __MOUNTAIN GOAT__   (ANSWERS MAY VARY)
5. __GOPHER AND/OR BISON__
6. What is a "bison"?
   __AN ANIMAL THAT LOOKS LIKE A BUFFALO__

7. What word means "an uncle or aunt's child"?
   (A. cousin)   B. camera   C. gopher
8. What would be a good title for this story?
   A. The Black Hills
   B. Winona's Cousin
   (C. Winona and Wapi Take Animal Photos)

Find it: Find South Dakota on a map of the United States.
Draw it: Draw a picture of an animal you might see in your state.

Worksheet 47

Name _____ Standard: Narrative Comprehension

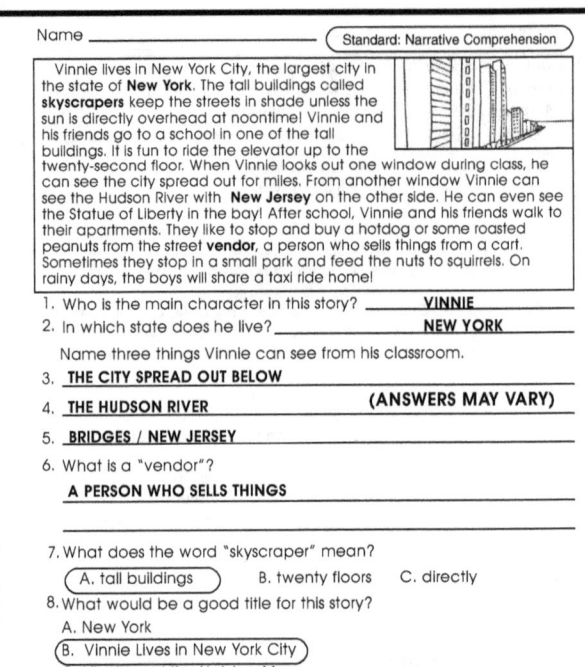

Vinnie lives in New York City, the largest city in the state of **New York**. The tall buildings called **skyscrapers** keep the streets in shade unless the sun is directly overhead at noontime! Vinnie and his friends go to a school in one of the tall buildings. It is fun to ride the elevator up to the twenty-second floor. When Vinnie looks out one window during class, he can see the city spread out for miles. From another window Vinnie can see the Hudson River with **New Jersey** on the other side. He can even see the Statue of Liberty in the bay! After school, Vinnie and his friends walk to their apartments. They like to stop and buy a hotdog or some roasted peanuts from the street **vendor**, a person who sells things from a cart. Sometimes they stop in a small park and feed the nuts to squirrels. On rainy days, the boys will share a taxi ride home!

1. Who is the main character in this story? __VINNIE__
2. In which state does he live? __NEW YORK__

Name three things Vinnie can see from his classroom.
3. __THE CITY SPREAD OUT BELOW__
4. __THE HUDSON RIVER__   (ANSWERS MAY VARY)
5. __BRIDGES / NEW JERSEY__
6. What is a "vendor"?
   __A PERSON WHO SELLS THINGS__

7. What does the word "skyscraper" mean?
   (A. tall buildings)   B. twenty floors   C. directly
8. What would be a good title for this story?
   A. New York
   (B. Vinnie Lives in New York City)
   C. Vinnie and the Hotdog Man

Find it: Find New York and New Jersey on a map of the United States.
Think about it: If you could visit New York City, what would you most like to see?

Worksheet 48

Name _____ Standard: Narrative Comprehension

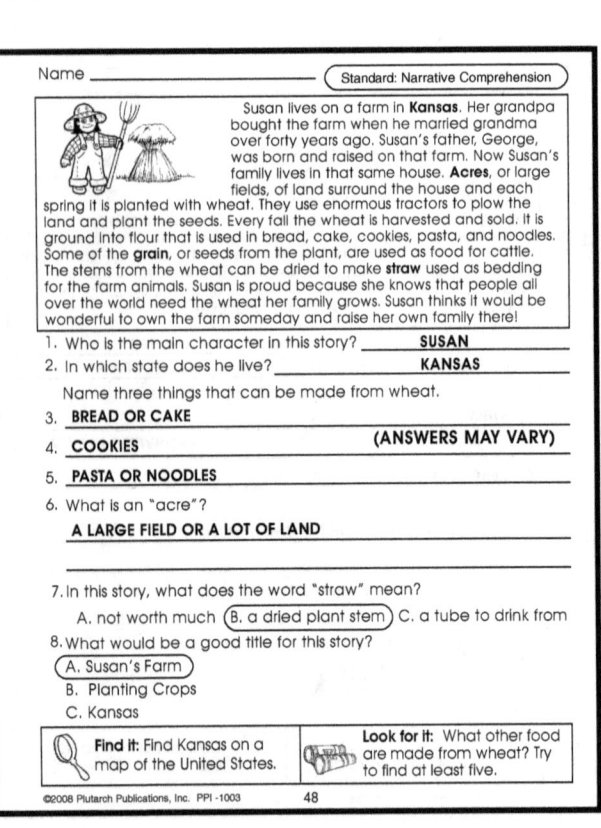

Susan lives on a farm in **Kansas**. Her grandpa bought the farm when he married grandma over forty years ago. Susan's father, George, was born and raised on that farm. Now Susan's family lives in that same house. **Acres**, or large fields, of land surround the house and each spring it is planted with wheat. They use enormous tractors to plow the land and plant the seeds. Every fall the wheat is harvested and sold. It is ground into flour that is used in bread, cake, cookies, pasta, and noodles. Some of the **grain**, or seeds from the plant, are used as food for cattle. The stems from the wheat can be dried to make **straw** used as bedding for the farm animals. Susan is proud because she knows that people all over the world need the wheat her family grows. Susan thinks it would be wonderful to own the farm someday and raise her own family there!

1. Who is the main character in this story? __SUSAN__
2. In which state does he live? __KANSAS__

Name three things that can be made from wheat.
3. __BREAD OR CAKE__
4. __COOKIES__   (ANSWERS MAY VARY)
5. __PASTA OR NOODLES__
6. What is an "acre"?
   __A LARGE FIELD OR A LOT OF LAND__

7. In this story, what does the word "straw" mean?
   A. not worth much   (B. a dried plant stem)   C. a tube to drink from
8. What would be a good title for this story?
   (A. Susan's Farm)
   B. Planting Crops
   C. Kansas

Find it: Find Kansas on a map of the United States.
Look for it: What other food are made from wheat? Try to find at least five.

Worksheet 49

Name _____ Standard: Narrative Comprehension

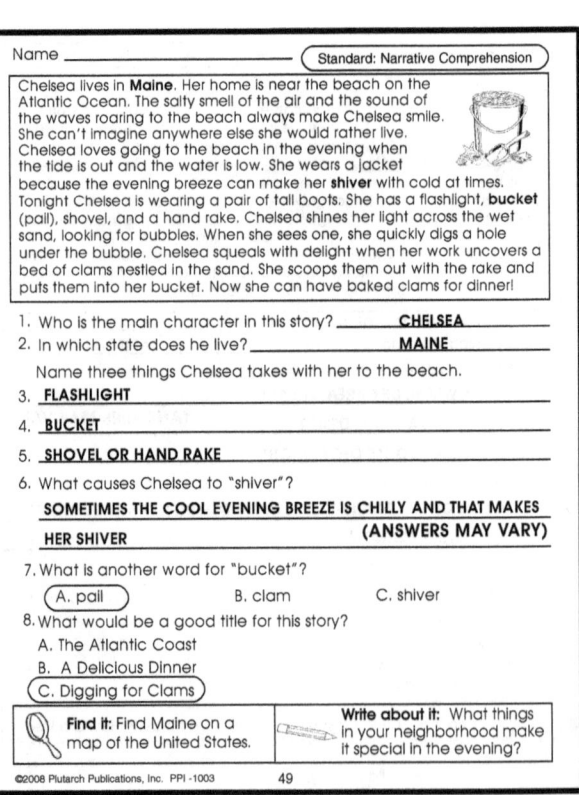

Chelsea lives in **Maine**. Her home is near the beach on the Atlantic Ocean. The salty smell of the air and the sound of the waves roaring to the beach always make Chelsea smile. She can't imagine anywhere else she would rather live. Chelsea loves going to the beach in the evening when the tide is out and the water is low. She wears a jacket because the evening breeze can make her **shiver** with cold at times. Tonight Chelsea is wearing a pair of tall boots. She has a flashlight, **bucket** (pail), shovel, and a hand rake. Chelsea shines her light across the wet sand, looking for bubbles. When she sees one, she quickly digs a hole under the bubble. Chelsea squeals with delight when her work uncovers a bed of clams nestled in the sand. She scoops them out with the rake and puts them into her bucket. Now she can have baked clams for dinner!

1. Who is the main character in this story? __CHELSEA__
2. In which state does he live? __MAINE__

Name three things Chelsea takes with her to the beach.
3. __FLASHLIGHT__
4. __BUCKET__
5. __SHOVEL OR HAND RAKE__
6. What causes Chelsea to "shiver"?
   __SOMETIMES THE COOL EVENING BREEZE IS CHILLY AND THAT MAKES__
   __HER SHIVER__   (ANSWERS MAY VARY)

7. What is another word for "bucket"?
   (A. pail)   B. clam   C. shiver
8. What would be a good title for this story?
   A. The Atlantic Coast
   B. A Delicious Dinner
   (C. Digging for Clams)

Find it: Find Maine on a map of the United States.
Write about it: What things in your neighborhood make it special in the evening?

ANSWER KEYS: 50, 51, 52, 53

Name _____ Standard: Narrative Comprehension

Clyde and his family live in the Blue Ridge Mountains of **Kentucky**. His father is a ranch hand for a huge horse farm. One night Clyde's father woke him and told him to get dressed. One of the **mares** (female horses) had just given birth to a new **foal**, or baby horse. Clyde was dressed and ready to go in just a few minutes. As Clyde and his dad drove up to the **stable**, or barn where the animals are kept, they could see the vet had already arrived. The stable was warm and Clyde could hear the other horses making soft noises as their sleep was disturbed by the visitors. When he looked into the stall, Clyde could see the baby horse next to its mother. The foal was already trying to stand up on its long, shaky legs. After three more tries, the foal got to its feet! In only a few more minutes it was able to walk a few feet to its mother. Clyde was sure he would never forget this night!

1. Who is the main character in this story? __**CLYDE**__
2. In which state does he live? __**KENTUCKY**__

Tell three things Clyde saw after he went into the stable.

3. __**THE FOAL WAS NEXT TO ITS MOTHER**__
4. __**THE FOAL TRIED TO STAND UP**__   (ANSWERS MAY VARY)
5. __**THE FOAL STOOD UP AND WALKED TO ITS MOTHER**__
6. What is a "stable"?
   __**A BARN THAT IS USED AS A HOME FOR ANIMALS**__

7. What does the word "mare" mean?
   A. soft noises   B. foal   (**C. female horse**)

8. What would be a good title for this story?
   (**A. A New Foal**)
   B. Clyde and His Father
   C. Clyde's Horses

Find it: Find Kentucky on a map of the United States.
Look for it: Read a book about horses. Find three facts you didn't know.

©2008 Plutarch Publications, Inc. PPI-1003   50

Name _____ Standard: Narrative Comprehension

It was an exciting day for Inola. She lived on the Nantahala River on the eastern **border**, or edge, of **North Carolina**. As Inola grew up, she spent many summer days splashing in the **shallow** (not very deep) water of the river near her home. She learned to fish in that river and enjoyed eating the rainbow trout that she caught. As she grew older, Inola learned to swim in the deeper water. Now she was ready for the best adventure of all. Inola was going on her first whitewater rafting trip! She had watched the big yellow rafts and listened to the people laugh and have a good time as they floated by. She knew that she would go over a few small waterfalls made by sudden drops in the river. She knew that many rafters tipped over or fell into the chilly water, but that didn't scare her. She was excited! Today it would be her turn, and she could hardly wait!

1. Who is the main character in this story? __**INOLA**__
2. In which state does he live? __**NORTH CAROLINA**__

Name three things Inola did in the river as she grew up.

3. __**SPLASHED IN THE WATER**__
4. __**LEARNED TO FISH**__
5. __**LEARNED TO SWIM**__
6. What is a "border"?
   __**A BORDER IS THE EDGE OF SOMETHING**__   (ANSWERS MAY VARY)

7. What does the word "shallow" mean?
   (**A. not deep**)   B. deep   C. colorful fish

8. What would be a good title for this story?
   A. Fishing in the River
   (**B. Inola's Special Day**)
   C. Rafting and Swimming

Find it: Find North Carolina on a map of the United States.
Draw it: What one thing would you like to do someday? Draw a picture of it.

©2008 Plutarch Publications, Inc. PPI-1003   51

Name _____ Standard: Expository Comprehension

Inventions

Early man did not have things like lights, boats, glass, or money. Everything we use each day was an **invention** (something made from an idea). We have socks because someone thought about covering their cold feet with a piece of cloth. They sewed the sock in the shape of a foot and it kept their toes toasty. An invention was born! Many inventions are things that were **necessary**, or needed, and people made them. Other inventions were wild ideas that few could even **imagine**, or see in their mind. For example, capturing sound and sending it through wires was an impossible idea until 1875 when Alexander Graham Bell found a way to do it. Today most of the people in the world have used a telephone, and many of us carry one right in our pocket! Not every idea will become an invention, but there could be no inventions without ideas!

Name seven inventions you use every day (not the ones in the story).

1. __**PENCIL**__
2. __**POTS AND PANS**__
3. __**COMPUTER**__
4. __**AUTOMOBILE**__
5. __**TELEVISION**__
6. __**RADIO**__   (ANSWERS WILL VARY)
7. __**STOVE**__

8. What is another word for "necessary"?
   A. idea   (**B. needed**)   C. impossible

9. What does the word "imagine" mean?
   __**TO SEE SOMETHING IN YOUR MIND**__

10. Who invented the telephone and in what year?
    __**ALEXANDER GRAHAM BELL IN 1875**__

 Think about it: Copy the list of inventions you named above. Why do you think each was necessary? What would life be like without each of them?

©2008 Plutarch Publications, Inc. PPI-1003   52

Name _____ Standard: Expository Comprehension

Up, Up, and Away!

The Aztecs were the first known people to use balloons. They cleaned bladders taken from cats, sewed them with a vegetable thread, and blew them into different shapes. Many cultures, such as the Eskimo and Indians, also played with bladder balloons. In 1783, two frenchmen made a 35 foot balloon of waxed paper and warmed the air in it, causing the balloon to rise. This was the invention of the "hot air" balloon. With the invention of rubber, balloons became easier to make. In 1824, rubber balloons were used in experiments with gases like **hydrogen**. These gases were lighter than air, allowing balloons to rise high into the sky without having to warm them. By 1889, people in the United States who enjoyed playing with these toys, could buy balloons for about four cents each. **Latex**, a type of stretchy rubber, was used in 1931.

1. What is the title of this story? __**UP, UP, AND AWAY**__
2. What is "hydrogen"? __**A GAS THAT IS LIGHTER THAN AIR**__

Name three cultures that made bladder balloons.

3. __**AZTEC**__
4. __**ESKIMO**__
5. __**INDIANS**__

6. What product is a type of stretchy rubber?
   A. hydrogen   (**B. latex**)   C. waxed paper

7. What was used to sew bladder balloons? __**VEGETABLE THREAD**__
8. In what year did balloons cost four cents? __**1889**__

The story lists four things balloons were made from. List three:

9. __**ANIMAL BLADDERS**__
10. __**WAXED PAPER**__
11. __**RUBBER OR LATEX**__

 Do it: Blow up a balloon and examine it. Can you make one of your own? Try different materials and see if you can make a balloon. What works? What doesn't work?

©2008 Plutarch Publications, Inc. PPI-1003   53

ANSWER KEYS: 54, 55, 56, 57

The Can Opener

The tin can, first used in 1810, was a good way to **preserve** food (keep it fresh). Cans were a good way to carry food for soldiers and travelers and they kept the food fresh for many months. Those cans were very thick and had to be opened with a hammer or the end of the soldier's rifle. This was messy and sometimes dangerous because of the sharp, ragged edges on the can. Soon cans were made thinner and were much easier to open. In 1858, Ezra Warner invented the first can opener. He got a **patent** for it, which is proof of legal ownership for an invention. His can opener had a sharp edge which was pushed into the can. The other end of the can opener, which looked like a hook, was then used to saw around the edge of the lid. In the 1870's, William Lyman designed a can opener with a cutting wheel, just like the ones we use today.

1. What is the title of this story? **THE CAN OPENER**
2. What does the word "patent" mean? **LEGAL PROOF OF OWNERSHIP FOR AN INVENTION**

Name two ways that thick cans were opened.
3. **WITH A HAMMER**
4. **WITH THE END OF A RIFLE**

6. What does the word "preserve" mean?
   (A. keep safe)   B. dangerous   C. ragged
7. What made cans easier to open? **THEY WERE MADE THINNER**
8. Who invented the 1870 can opener? **WILLIAM LYMAN**
9. Why were the first cans so difficult to open? **THEY WERE THICK**
10. In your own words, explain how Ezra Warner's can opener worked.
    A SHARP EDGE MADE A HOLE IN THE LID OF THE CAN. A HOOKED END CUT OPEN THE LID. (ANSWERS WILL VARY)

Share it: Use the newspaper, magazines, and the computer to find different types of can openers. Make a poster that shows how they have changed over the years.

Wash Those Dishes!

The first machine invented to wash dishes was built in 1850. The wooden box splashed water on the dishes, but it didn't clean them well. A **wealthy** (rich) woman, Josephine Cochrane, waited for someone to invent a dishwasher that would do the job. No one did, so she decided to invent one herself! First, she designed wire racks to hold the dishes. Second, the racks were slipped inside **boiler**, or heater, with a water wheel. Third, the wheel shot hot, soapy water on the dishes. Josephine's dishwasher worked well, so she patented it. In 1893 she **displayed**, or showed, it to the public for the first time at the World's Fair and she won an award. Hotels and restaurants were very interested and the Cochrane Dishwasher was a hit. In the 1950's it became popular to have a dishwasher in the home, and today many homes have one.

1. What is the title of this story? **WASH THOSE DISHES!**
2. What does it mean to be "wealthy"? **RICH OR HAVE MONEY**

List the three steps to using the Cochrane Dishwasher:
3. **PUT DISHES IN THE WIRE RACK**
4. **PUT THE RACK INSIDE A WHEEL**
5. **SHOOT HOT, SOAPY WATER ON THE DISHES**

6. What does it mean to "display" something?
   A. wash it   B. invent it   (C. show it)
7. What is a "boiler"? **A HEATER**
8. In what year was the first dishwasher invented? **1850**

What two types of businesses were the first to use the dishwasher?
9. **HOTELS**
10. **RESTAURANTS**
11. When did dishwashers become popular in homes? **THE 1950'S**

Think about it: Which do you like best, washing dishes by hand or putting them in the dishwasher? What makes hand washing better? What makes using a dishwasher better?

Invented or Discovered?

Joshua Lionel Cowen, the inventor of the flashlight in 1989, owned a battery company. He invented the flashlight totally by **accident**, not on purpose! Joshua wanted a lamp to light up potted plants in his store. He **fashioned**, or made, a long metal tube and attached a small lightbulb. Batteries kept it lit for thirty days. He sold this invention in his battery store, and people found it much more useful as a portable light, one that could be carried anywhere without wires attached. Conrad Hubert, a sales person at the store, gave the flashlight its name. The flashlight became very popular and soon Mr. Cowen was very rich. In 1900, he wanted to advertise a sale item in his front window. He thought a tiny car that ran on a track might catch people's attention. The car didn't work well, so he made a tiny train instead. Not many people wanted the sale item, but everyone loved the train, so the Lionel Train Company was born. It still makes trains today!

1. What is the title of this story? **INVENTED OR DISCOVERED?**
2. What is an "accident"? **SOMETHING NOT DONE ON PURPOSE**

Name three parts of the flashlight:
3. **A METAL TUBE**
4. **A SMALL LIGHTBULB**
5. **BATTERIES**

6. The first toy train was invented for what use?
   A. a new toy   (B. a store display)   C. to light up plants
7. What was the first flashlight supposed to be? **A LIGHT FOR PLANTS**
8. In what year was the toy train invented? **1900**
9. Who gave the flashlight its name? **CONRAD HUBERT**
10. In your own words, tell how the toy train was invented:
    MR. COWEN WANTED HIS WINDOW TO BE NOTICED. HE MADE A TINY CAR THAT RAN ON A TRACK. IT DIDN'T WORK SO HE MADE A TRAIN INSTEAD. (ANSWERS WILL VARY)

Think about it: Can you remember a time when something you did by accident ended up being a good thing? Share your story with three other people and listen to their stories.

Cut the Grass

Yards with trimmed and tidy grass were first found in France in the 1700's. People liked the neat **lawns** and soon the idea spread to the rest of the world. The first "lawn mowers" were actually animals that **grazed**, or ate the grass during the day. That kept the grass short, but it wasn't even and the animals left the lawn messy. Tools like scissors and **sickles** (curved blades with handles) were used for many years, but they didn't cut evenly. In 1830, Edwin Budding put blades around a **cylinder**, or wide tube, and attached wheels and a long handle. Horses pulled the mower and the blades clipped the grass evenly. This worked well, but the horses had to wear leather booties so they didn't leave hoof prints on the lawn. In 1870, Elwood McGuire made a lawnmower that was light enough for humans to push. It left the lawn even and without footprints!

1. What is the title of this story? **CUT THE GRASS**
2. What is a "sickle"? **A CURVED BLADE WITH A HANDLE**

The story tells three ways lawns have been cut. List them:
3. **ANIMALS ATE GRASS TO KEEP IT SHORT** (ANSWERS WILL VARY)
4. **HORSES PULLED BLADES ATTACHED TO WHEELS**
5. **HUMANS PUSHED A LIGHTER LAWNMOWER**

6. What does the word "graze" mean?
   (A. eat grass)   B. tidy   C. cover with sugar
7. In what year was the horse-pulled mower invented? **1830**
8. In what year was the human push-mower invented? **1870**

List three reasons why animals were not good for mowing lawns:
9. **THEY LEFT THE LAWN MESSY**
10. **THEY DID NOT CUT GRASS EVENLY** (ANSWERS WILL VARY)
11. **THEY LEFT HOOF PRINTS ON THE LAWN**

Compare it: Find a picture of a human push mower used in the 1950's. Compare it to the lawnmower used today. How are they alike? How are they different?

ANSWER KEYS: 58, 59, 60. 61

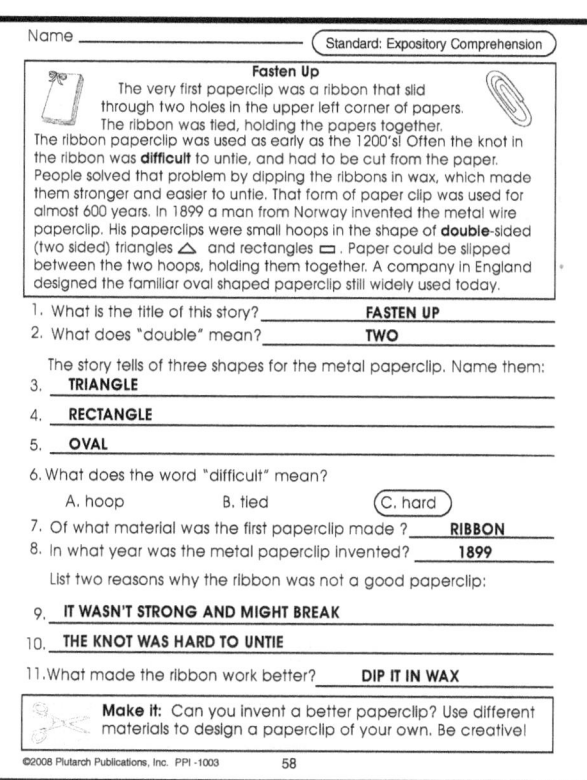

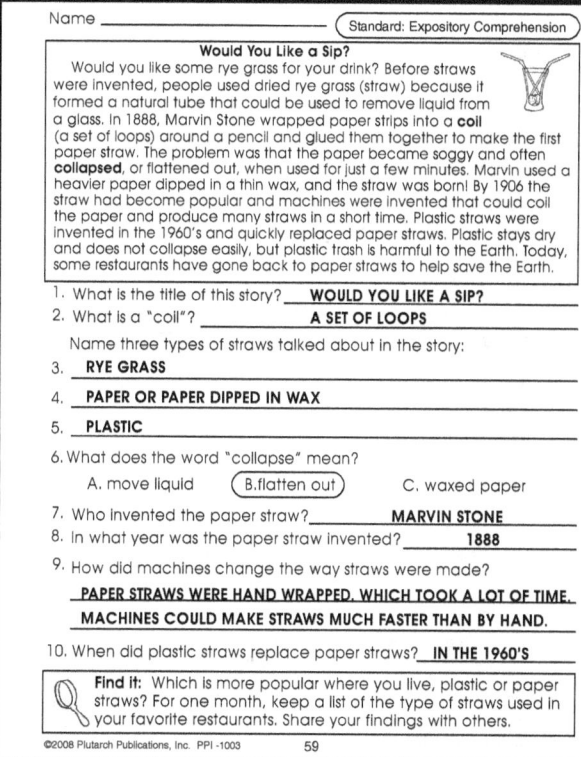

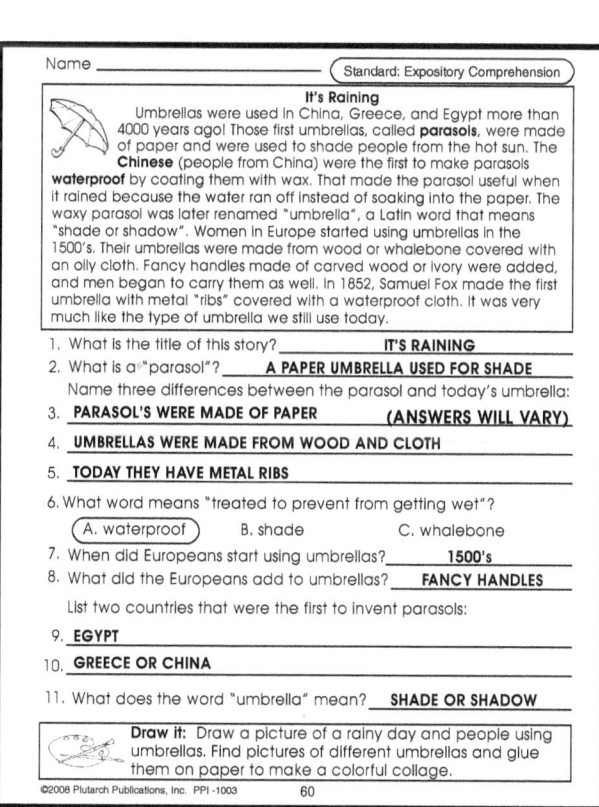

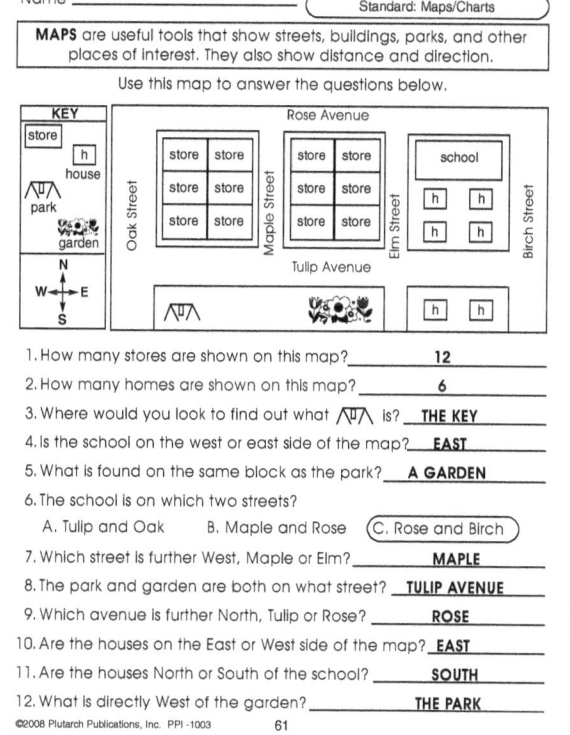

ANSWER KEYS: 62, 63, 64, 65

Name _____ Standard: Maps/Charts

A **CHART** is a table that gives information in a list, making it easier to read and understand.

The Tyson family planted a vegetable garden. Each person kept a record of how many seeds they planted. Father made a chart from the information. Use this chart to answer the questions below.

	Corn	Lettuce	Tomatoes	Onions	Carrots
Jerry	3	1	7	1	5
Beth	5	0	2	0	3
Marvin	4	2	1	1	4
Mother	4	5	4	1	5
Father	8	4	4	3	4

1. How many people planted seeds? **5**
2. Name the people: **JERRY, BETH, MARVIN, MOTHER, FATHER**
3. Name the kinds of seeds that were planted: **CORN, LETTUCE, TOMATOES, ONIONS, CARROTS**
4. Who planted the least tomatoes? **MARVIN**
5. Jerry planted 7 seeds of which vegetable? **TOMATOES**
6. Which vegetable did Father plant most? **CORN**
7. Which two vegetables do you think Beth does not like very much?
   (A. lettuce & onions)   B. corn & beans   C. lettuce & carrots
8. Who planted the most onions? **FATHER**
9. Who planted the least number of carrots? **BETH**
10. Which two people each planted four corn seeds?
    A. Marvin & Father   B. Mother & Father   (C. Mother & Marvin)
11. Which vegetable had the least number of seeds planted in all?
    A. corn   (B. onions)   C. lettuce

©2008 Plutarch Publications, Inc. PPI-1003   62

Name _____ Standard: Maps/Charts

A **TIMELINE** is a chart that shows the order in which events happened.
Read Olive and Ryan's stories. Put the letter of each event on the blank under the timeline to show the proper order of their events.

Olive had a busy day last Saturday. She got up at 6:30 because there was much to do. She fixed pancakes for the family breakfast and they ate at 7:00. By 7:30 Olive finished washing and drying the dishes. At 8:00, Olive put on her work clothes and helped mother dust the house. At 8:30 she went outside and helped Father weed the garden. They finished at 9:00 and Olive sat on the swing to take a short rest.

  A. finished dishes
  B. put on work clothes
  C. got out of bed
  D. sat down to rest
  E. weeded the garden
  F. ate breakfast

6:30	7:00	7:30	8:00	8:30	9:00
C	F	A	B	E	D

Ryan wrote a story telling about the important things that happened in his life. He got his first puppy when he was three years old. Ryan started school at five years old. When he was only one, Ryan took his first ride in an airplane. His favorite birthday was at the zoo when he turned six. His sister, Ruth, was born when he was two. Best of all, Ryan went to Colorado and saw the Grand Canyon when he was four.

  A. got a puppy
  B. started school
  C. first ride in an airplane
  D. birthday party at the zoo
  E. sister was born
  F. took a trip to the Grand Canyon

1 year	2 years	3 years	4 years	5 years	6 years
C	E	A	F	B	D

©2008 Plutarch Publications, Inc. PPI-1003   63

Name _____ Standard: Forms/Signs

Signs are an important part of our lives. They give us information, keep us safe, and help us find places. Below are six signs we see every day.

A   B   C   D   E   F

Read each sentence below. Decide which of the above signs you might find in that situation. Write the letter of that sign on the blank.

E 1. You are on a busy street near a school. Children are waiting at the corner. A crossing guard is helping them cross the street to get to school. Which sign would you see?

A 2. You are in a restaurant and you have had two glasses of water. You need to go to the restroom. Which sign would you look for?

B 3. You are in a car going to the mall on the other side of the city. You see train tracks crossing the road. Which sign would you most likely see?

D 4. Your mother is driving you to your friend's house. You come to a busy street corner that has no traffic light. Which sign would help you get safely through the busy street corner?

F 5. In the car on your way to the beach you see a path crossing the road. People riding bikes and skating along the path need to cross the road. Which sign would you see?

C 6. Which sign would you probably see in all of these places: hospital; school; restaurant; courtroom; theater; library; playground; and museum.

©2008 Plutarch Publications, Inc. PPI-1003   64

Name _____ Standard: Forms/Signs

Many times in your life you will have to fill out forms. You need to fill out forms for things like getting a job, seeing a doctor, or buying a car.

Felix Sanchez is eight years old. His pet, a dog named Scruffy, is two years old. Scruffy is a male boxer. Felix and his father, Carlos Sanchez, took Scruffy to the vet, Dr. Bellos, for a check-up. Felix had to fill out a form before the vet could look at Scruffy.

1. Owner's name: _____
2. Owner's address: _____
3. Owner's phone number: _____
4. Type of pet: _____   5. Name of pet: _____
6. Age of pet: _____   7. Sex of pet: _____
8. Color of pet: _____
9. Has this pet visited the vet before? _____

1. From this form, will the vet know the pet's name? **YES**
2. Does the form give the vet's name? **NO**
3. What should Felix write on line 1?
   A. Scruffy   (B. Felix Sanchez)   C. Dr. Bellos
4. From this form, will the vet know how old the pet is? **YES**
5. From this form, will the vet know how many years Felix has owned Scruffy? **NO**
6. What should Felix write on line 6?
   (A. two)   B. seven   C. eight
7. From this card, will the vet know that the pet is a dog? **YES**
8. What WOULDN'T Felix write on line 8?
   A. brown   (B. 555-1103)   C. black and white
9. What should Felix write on line 7?
   (A. male)   B. female   C. dog

©2008 Plutarch Publications, Inc. PPI-1003   65

ANSWER KEYS: 66, 67, 68, 69

Page 66

Name _____ Standard: Forms/Signs

Many times in your life you will have to fill out forms. You need to fill out forms to get a job, go to the doctor, buy a car, and start at a new school.

Read the story below and use the information given to fill out the form.

Mr. Steve Townsend is a policeman. He got a new job in another city, bought a house, and moved his family there in June. His wife, Mindy, got a job as a teacher at Bedford Middle School. His children, Mark and Martha, are in the third grade at Parker School. Their new address is 107 Parkway Place, Dayton, Ohio, 49316. Their new phone number is 555-1742. Mark found a library only two blocks from his new home. The librarian asked him to fill out a form to get a new library card. Can you help Mark fill out the form?

1. Name: **TOWNSEND** (Last)   **MARK** (First)
2. Address: **107** (Number)   **PARKWAY PLACE** (Street)
   DAYTON (City)   **OHIO** (State)   **49316** (Zip Code)
3. Phone number: **555-1742**
4. Name of your school: **PARKER SCHOOL**
5. Grade in school: **THIRD**
6. Name of parents or guardian: **STEVE AND MINDY TOWNSEND**
7. Job of parents or guardian: **POLICEMAN AND TEACHER**

Page 67

Name _____ Standard: Dictionary/Glossary

Words in a dictionary or glossary are listed in **alphabetical order** (ABC).

Can you put these two groups of words in alphabetical order?

Group 1: limp, damp, hatch, guest, banana, admire, coast, inch, mistake, jolly, knife, enjoy, fancy

Group 2: unwrap, wobble, nature, tomato, zip, visitor, onion, power, reason, x-ray, safety, yawn, quarter

1. ADMIRE
2. BANANA
3. COAST
4. DAMP
5. ENJOY
6. FANCY
7. GUEST
8. HATCH
9. INCH
10. JOLLY
11. KNIFE
12. LIMP
13. MISTAKE

1. NATURE
2. ONION
3. POWER
4. QUARTER
5. REASON
6. SAFETY
7. TOMATO
8. UNWRAP
9. VISITOR
10. WOBBLE
11. X-RAY
12. YAWN
13. ZIP

Page 68

Name _____ Standard: Dictionary/Glossary

A dictionary lists words in alphabetical order. It gives the **pronunciation** (how to say it), part of speech, and **definition**, or meaning.

Use this page from the dictionary to answer the questions below.

fail (fāl) *verb.* to not succeed or miss doing what was to be done
faint (fānt) *adjective.* to be weak, not strong, or unclear
fake (fāk) *verb.* to make something seem real in order to fool others
fame (fām) *noun.* being well known or much talked about
fellow (fel'o) *noun.* a man or boy
fierce (firs) *adjective.* wild or cruel
flare (fler) *verb.* to spread outward like a bell
fuss (fus) *noun.* too much bother or worry over a small thing

1. What is a *fake* jewel?
   A. a jewel that isn't real
   B. something valuable
   C. a diamond

2. Which word means "male"?
   A. fame
   B. fellow
   C. flare

3. Which word is a verb?
   A. faint
   B. fierce
   C. flare

4. What is a "definition"?
   A. how to say a word
   B. the meaning of a word
   C. the part of speech

5. Which word means "wild"?
   A. fake
   B. fame
   C. fierce

6. What part of speech is *fail*?
   A. verb
   B. adjective
   C. noun

7. What is a *fuss*?
   A. a long piece of string
   B. crying
   C. a big deal over nothing

8. Which person would have *fame*?
   A. a shy person
   B. a movie star
   C. a rabbit

Page 69

Name _____ Standard: Dictionary/Glossary

A **GLOSSARY** is like a dictionary of special terms found at the back of a textbook like Science or Social Studies. The page number where the word is used in the book is given in parentheses ( ).

Read the glossary and use it to answer the questions below.

Glossary of Landforms:
canyon (22) - narrow valley with high steep sides
continent (18) - a very large mass of land covering the Earth
gulf (16) - part of the ocean that is almost surrounded by land
lake (13) - a large body of inland water
mountain (23) - large mass of land that rises above the surrounding land
ocean (12) - large body of water that covers most of the Earth
peak (23) - the pointed top of a mountain
peninsula (19) - a piece of land surrounded by water on three sides
plain (21) - large area of level or flat ground
stream (17) - a body of water that flows across the land

1. Are the words listed in alphabetical order? **YES**
2. What group of words are listed in this glossary?
   A. landforms   B. math words   C. oceans
3. What word means "the point at the top of a mountain"?
   A. canyon   **B. peak**   C. plain
4. On what page would the book talk about oceans?
   A. 11   **B. 12**   C. 18
5. Is a peninsula made of land or water? **LAND**
6. Which two words can be found on page 23?
   A. ocean - stream   B. peak - canyon   **C. mountain - peak**
7. Which type of land is a large flat area?
   A. canyon   B. mountain   **C. plain**
8. Which type of water can be found inland?
   A. lake   B. gulf   C. ocean

www.ingramcontent.com/pod-product-compliance
Lightning Source LLC
Chambersburg PA
CBHW081018040426
42444CB00014B/3256